This book belongs to

....

At the Height of the Moon

A Book of Bedtime Poetry and Art

Edited by Annette Roeder,
Alison Baverstock,
and Matt Cunningham

PRESTEL

Munich · London · New York

Table of Contents

Twilight

Dreamland

Moonlit Menagerie

Creepy Crawlies and Things that Go Bump in the Night

Minds Ablaze

Midnight and Magic

ALICE IN WONDERLAND

by George Dunlop Leslie

Hush, now. Listen …

HERE IT COMES, SOFTLY—LOOK!—IN SHIFTING, YAWNING, SLEEPILY STRETCHING SHADOWS.

EVENING. TWILIGHT. NIGHT.

(Listen⸮ *Look*⸮ What's there to look at when night-time comes⸮ The whole point of the night is it's dark. I can't see a thing!)

Then we need to look more closely, don't we⸮ With bright keen eyes. Like artists do …

All through the years they've been at it—artists, enchanted. Painters mix vermilions and cobalt blues, lemon yellows and copper greens to capture the night on canvas, in all its subtle hues. Poets weave night's wonders through their lines; writers, into stories rich with magic; composers, into marvellous moonlit melodies. Artists know that night isn't just darkness. These are the hours when everything's transformed: silence soars, the sweat on our skin turns pinprick cool, our homes get cosier; some say fairy tales come true. Outside, nocturnal creatures go about their secret business, while here on the pillow—what's this⸮—a nightmare, scuttling, with a spider's eyes! But don't worry. If at times the night makes thoughts grow heavy, a quick shuffle in bed makes them sillier too—and love beats harder beneath the light of the moon.

And then come dreams …

As colourful as this book! The following pages are filled with paintings, poems, stories, songs and much more. Some are famous, some are less well-known, but all capture in their different ways the charms that come with nightfall. In Germany, the book has already been welcomed with joy; we're delighted to present this new version, created especially for English-speaking audiences. The images remain the same, while the words are new. All were chosen with love. SO CUDDLE UP, MARVEL, LAUGH, SING, PEEK THROUGH YOUR FINGERS IF YOU MUST …

BUT MOST OF ALL, LISTEN! LOOK…

HERE COMES THE NIGHT.

Annette Roeder
Alison Baverstock
Matt Cunningham

LADY IN A GARDEN BY MOONLIGHT
Detail
by John Atkinson Grimshaw

Twilight

REIMAGINED GARDEN:
ON JOHN SARGENT'S *CARNATION, LILY, LILY, ROSE*

Look, Polly, look
how our lanterns blush –
the skipping half-light, such
almost like moons
but not quite –

and all around us
drowsy lilies with long anthers,
grass brushing against our knees.
The perfumed air,
the garden's ours,
and the queen bees rule.

Dolly I've done mine now,
I'm pleased
even if the wind blows.
Here roses don't stop growing
and lilies last forever.
Let's hurry up
it's almost time.

Oh the Barnhard girls,
light on their slender arms,
their rustling cotton sleeves,
that summer they never
grow out of.
So much to fill,
so little time before the sun goes.

If only you'd let me finish my song.
Would you let me finish my song?
Carnation, lily, lily, rose,
hands lily white, lips
plump and juicy red.
Time on their napes
and soft elbows
but none for me.
Where is my Cotswolds of yesterday?

Jennifer Wong

CARNATION, LILY, LILY, ROSE
Detail
by John Singer Sargent

12

THE OCEAN

The Ocean has its silent caves,
Deep, quiet, and alone;
Though there be fury on the waves,
Beneath them there is none.

The awful spirits of the deep
Hold their communion there;
And there are those for whom we weep,
The young, the bright, the fair.

Calmly the wearied seamen rest
Beneath their own blue sea.
The ocean solitudes are blest,
For there is purity.

The earth has guilt, the earth has care,
Unquiet are its graves;
But peaceful sleep is ever there,
Beneath the dark blue waves.

Nathaniel Hawthorne

DREAMS

Here we are all, by day; by night we're hurl'd
By dreams, each one into a several world.

Robert Herrick

WATER LILIES

Detail
by Claude Monet

Preludes I

The winter evening settles down
With smell of steaks in passageways.
Six o'clock.
The burnt-out ends of smoky days.
And now a gusty shower wraps
The grimy scraps
Of withered leaves about your feet
And newspapers from vacant lots;
The showers beat
On broken blinds and chimney-pots,
And at the corner of the street
A lonely cab-horse steams and stamps.

And then the lighting of the lamps.

T. S. Eliot

The Little Dancers

LONELY, save for a few faint stars, the sky
Dreams; and lonely, below, the little street
Into its gloom retires, secluded and shy.
Scarcely the dumb roar enters this soft retreat;
And all is dark, save where come flooding rays
From a tavern window: there, to the brisk measure
Of an organ that down in an alley merrily plays,
Two children, all alone and no one by,
Holding their tatter'd frocks, through an airy maze
Of motion, lightly threaded with nimble feet,
Dance sedately: face to face they gaze,
Their eyes shining, grave with a perfect pleasure.

Laurence Binyon

The Houses of Parliament (Effect of Fog)

by Claude Monet

A night in June

The sun has long been set,
The stars are out by twos and threes,
The little birds are piping yet
Among the bushes and trees;
There's a cuckoo, and one or two thrushes,
And a far-off wind that rushes,
And a sound of water that gushes,
And the cuckoo's sovereign cry
Fills all the hollow of the sky.
Who would "go parading"
In London, "and masquerading,"
On such a night of June
With that beautiful soft half-moon,
And all these innocent blisses؟
On such a night as this is!

William Wordsworth

Spring Evening
Detail
by Henri Le Sidaner

TIRED TIM

POOR tired Tim! It's sad for him.
He lags the long bright morning through,
Ever so tired of nothing to do;
He moons and mopes the livelong day,
Nothing to think about, nothing to say;
Up to bed with his candle to creep,
Too tired to yawn; too tired to sleep:
Poor tired Tim! It's sad for him.

Walter de la Mare

SONG

Oh, baby, baby, baby dear,
We lie alone together here;
The snowy gown and cap and sheet
With lavender are fresh and sweet;
Through half-closed blinds the roses peer
To see and love you, baby dear.

We are so tired, we like to lie
Just doing nothing, you and I,
   Within the darkened quiet room.
      The sun sends dusk rays through the gloom,
         Which is no gloom since you are here,
         My little life, my baby dear.

      Soft sleepy mouth so vaguely pressed
         Against your new-made mother's breast,
         Soft little hands in mine I fold,
         Soft little feet I kiss and hold,
         Round soft smooth head and tiny ear,
         All mine, my own, my baby dear.

      And he we love is far away!
         But he will come some happy day,
         You need but me, and I can rest
         At peace with you beside me pressed.
      There are no questions, longings vain,
   No murmuring, nor doubt, nor pain,
Only content and we are here,
My baby dear.

Edith Nesbit

LATE RISER

by Theodor Alt

The Best Bedtime Hot Chocolate

Ingredients
for one person

1 cup of milk
3–4 teaspoons of
   cocoa powder
2 teaspoons of sugar
½ cup of whipping cream
A pinch of cinnamon
1 nougat praline
   (or a piece of
   chocolate nougat)

And for the grown-ups:
   a shot of hazelnut
   liqueur

Whisk the whipping cream until stiff
and set aside. While warming the
milk, whisk vigorously into a froth.
Then add the cocoa powder, sugar,
and cinnamon.

If you're old enough, and so inclined,
add the hazelnut liqueur. Pour the hot
chocolate into a mug and top it off
with a thick layer of whipped cream.
Sprinkle with nougat praline.

The best bedtime chocolate is served
with a glass of cold water.

Drink … have a story read to you …
brush your teeth well …

then off to bed!

The Chocolate Girl
by Jean-Étienne Liotard

THE REALLYREALLYREALLY TRULYTRUETRUTH ABOUT... TEDDY BEARS

EVERYBODY has a teddy.
Even if they say they don't, they do,
they're fibbing. Even kings, queens,

famous footballers, hairy rock stars
and busy teachers. Yours included.
And all those people on the telly. Them too.

And I'm sure even aliens have their own
equally cute, equally cuddly, equally
dog-eared, squished and dribbled-over

version of this classic soft toy. But why?
Well, why not? However old you are,
however grown up you may appear to be,

however important or bossy you may become,
in a hush of a moment every now and then,
you will still feel the need to open

the bedroom cupboard, remove
that little fuzzy bundle, and give it
a sniff and a kiss and a little snuggle.

James Carter

THE BEAR FAMILY
by Alexej von Jawlensky

MOONLIGHT AT THE PORT OF BOULOGNE

by Édouard Manet

O Captain! My Captain!

O Captain! my Captain! our fearful trip is done,
The ship has weather'd every rack, the prize we sought is won,
The port is near, the bells I hear, the people all exulting,
While follow eyes the steady keel, the vessel grim and daring;
 But O heart! heart! heart!
  O the bleeding drops of red,
   Where on the deck my Captain lies,
    Fallen cold and dead.

    O Captain! my Captain! rise up and hear the bells;
    Rise up—for you the flag is flung—for you the bugle trills,
    For you bouquets and ribbon'd wreaths—for you the shores a-crowding,
    For you they call, the swaying mass, their eager faces turning;
     Here Captain! dear father!
      This arm beneath your head!
       It is some dream that on the deck,
        You've fallen cold and dead.

My Captain does not answer, his lips are pale and still,
My father does not feel my arm, he has no pulse nor will,
The ship is anchor'd safe and sound, its voyage closed and done,
From fearful trip the victor ship comes in with object won;
 Exult O shores, and ring O bells!
  But I with mournful tread,
   Walk the deck my Captain lies,
    Fallen cold and dead.

Walt Whitman

GOLDEN SLUMBERS

Golden slumbers kiss your eyes,
Smiles awake you when you rise;
Sleep, pretty wantons, do not cry,
And I will sing a lullaby,
Rock them, rock them, lullaby.

Care is heavy, therefore sleep you,
You are care, and care must keep you;
Sleep, pretty wantons, do not cry,
And I will sing a lullaby,
Rock them, rock them, lullaby.

Thomas Dekker

Musical Angel

by Rosso Fiorentino

GOOD NIGHT!
GOOD NIGHT!

Papa, my mouth is tired.
My hands are tired.
Can you read the book to me?

I don't mind. I'll read and you
   can look at the pictures.
Or are your eyes tired too?

**My eyes are still awake
and my ears too!**

Alright then:
The dirt track shimmers
   and shines and whispers,
but **the snail** has long disappeared
   into its cozy house.
Good night!

ANIMAL PICTURE (LION)
by Hans Hoffmann

The flower meadow blooms and shines and smells,
but the bee has long put on its striped pajamas.
Good night!

The apple tree has pitched the apple far and laughs and
chuckles and waves, but the apple, weary from its flight,
lies soft and warm in the grass.
Good night!

The shrub in Australia shrinks and waits and says, "Now!"
but the kangaroo won't jump over it anymore. It wanted to
lull its babies to sleep and fell asleep too.
Good night!

The hoop in the circus makes itself big and stands on a
podium in the middle of the ring, but the lion is tired from the
drum roll and dreams of much different leaps.
Good night!

The river gurgles and ripples and wants to play, but the elephant
has already trumpeted its last jet of water into the air and is
rolling happily on its side.
Good night!

The gently rocking bowl on the floor is still half full,
 but **the cat** has long been purring quietly in its sleep.
Good night!

And that is how it is here, there, and everywhere.
The sea splashes on and **the bear** goes to sleep in its cave.
 The sky goes on forever, but **the birds in their nest** tuck
 their heads under their wings and rest.

And you?
Your little toe is still alive. Was there a movement there?
 But the tip of your nose is already asleep.
A quick kiss just before your lips go to sleep!
And now: Good night!

The book has been read, the pictures have been seen.
 Papa receives a quick kiss.

"Good night," whispers Lilli. There is hardly a sound.
 The father quietly closes the book, as quietly as a butterfly
 closes its wings.

Good night! **Good night!**

Heinz Janisch

THE COTTAGER TO HER INFANT

The days are cold, the nights are long,
The North wind sings a doleful song;
Then hush again upon my breast;
All merry things are now at rest,
　Save thee, my pretty love!

The kitten sleeps upon the hearth,
The crickets long have ceased their mirth;
There's nothing stirring in the house
Save one wee, hungry, nibbling mouse,
　Then why so busy thou?

Nay! start not at the sparkling light;
'Tis but the moon that shines so bright
　On the window-pane
　Bedropped with rain:

Then, little darling! sleep again,
And wake when it is day.

Dorothy Wordsworth

34

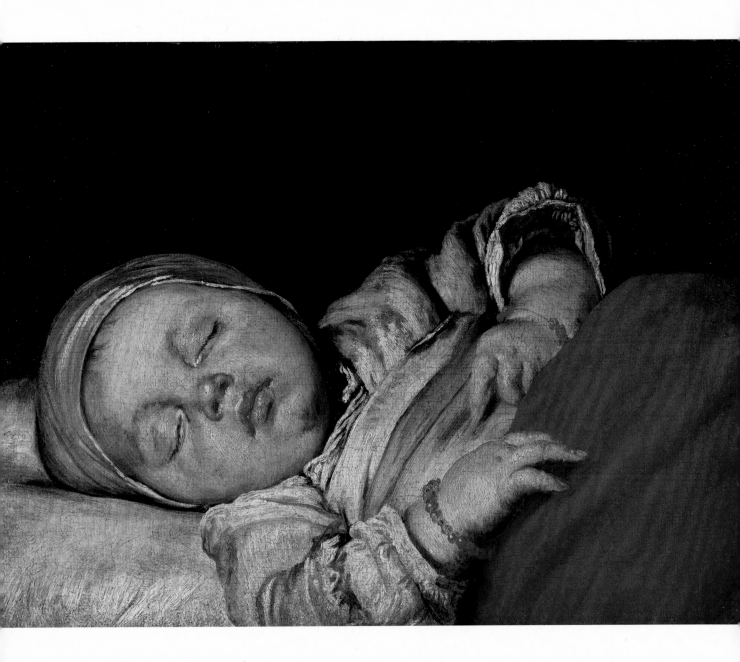

SLEEPING CHILD

by Bernardo Strozzi

TITANIA AND BOTTOM
from William Shakespeare's 'A Midsummer-Night's Dream'
by John Anster Fitzgerald

reamland

REMINISCENCES OF EARLY LIFE

And such are those that cheered the moonlight night,
When winter's mirth made up for winter's blight;
When bands of skaters cut the glassy plain,
Swift as the breeze flew o'er the bleak domain,
Avoiding, carefully, the gloomy shade,
Where lurked the treacherous, latent, watery glade;
And, wheeling proudly o'er the fettered deep,
Cried, "Thorn away," and slid with rapid sweep.
Oh! 'twas fine sport to stem the north-west wind,
And leave a rival scholar far behind,
To match good skaters and disdain to lag,
And beat the fleetest in the flying Tag,
While the stars twinkled coldly through the frost,
In the moon's brighter radiance almost lost.

Nor let the kindred pastimes be forgot,
That still endured, when fragile ice did not,
When the long hill, the level land below,
And the straight course were covered o'er with snow,
And iced, if possible, if not, well-trod,
And smoothed by sleds with runners iron-shod.
Methinks, I see the active, happy throng,
Urged by the cold to keep their bodies warm,
The fleet career, the look of keen delight,
The breath suspended by the downward flight,
The freight of laughing girls, a precious load,
Seldom allowed to grace the slippery road,
Conducted by some roguish timoneer,
Who loved a frolic as he loved to steer,
Skilled, when his vessel was descending swift,
To turn and land his cargo in a drift.

Anonymous

A Moonlit Winter Landscape with Skaters on a Frozen River

Detail
by Franz de Paula Ferg

THE DREAM

by Henri Rousseau

Rainforest

The forest drips and glows with green.
The tree-frog croaks his far-off song.
His voice is stillness, moss and rain
drunk from the forest ages long.

We cannot understand that call
unless we move into his dream,
where all is one and one is all
and frog and python are the same.

We with our quick dividing eyes
measure, distinguish and are gone.
The forest burns, the tree-frog dies,
yet one is all and all are one.

Judith Wright

The Tempest
Act III, Scene 2

Be not afeard; the isle is full of noises,
Sounds, and sweet airs, that give delight and hurt not.
Sometimes a thousand twangling instruments
Will hum about mine ears; and sometime voices
That, if I then had waked after long sleep,
Will make me sleep again; and then, in dreaming,
The clouds methought would open, and show riches
Ready to drop upon me, that when I waked
I cried to dream again.

William Shakespeare

THE FAIRIES

Up the airy mountain,
Down the rushy glen,
We daren't go a-hunting
For fear of little men;
Wee folk, good folk,
Trooping all together;
Green jacket, red cap,
And white owl's feather!

Down along the rocky shore
Some make their home;
They live on crispy pancakes
Of yellow tide-foam;
Some in the reeds
Of the black mountain lake,
With frogs for their watch-dogs,
All night awake.

High on the hill-top
The old King sits;
He is now so old and grey
He's nigh lost his wits.
With a bridge of white mist
Columbkill he crosses,
On his stately journeys
From Slieveleague to Rosses;
Or going up with the music
On cold starry nights,
To sup with the Queen
Of the gay Northern Lights.

They stole little Bridget
For seven years long;
When she came down again
Her friends were all gone.
They took her lightly back,
Between the night and morrow,
They thought that she was fast asleep,
But she was dead with sorrow.
They have kept her ever since
Deep within the lake,
On a bed of fig-leaves,
Watching till she wake.

By the craggy hill-side,
Through the mosses bare,
They have planted thorn-trees
For my pleasure here and there.
Is any man so daring
As dig them up in spite,
He shall find the thornies set
In his bed at night.

Up the airy mountain,
Down the rushy glen,
We daren't go a-hunting
For fear of little men;
Wee folk, good folk,
Trooping all together;
Green jacket, red cap,
And white owl's feather!

William Allingham

MIDSUMMER EVE
by Edward Robert Hughes

MODERN LOVE

It is summer, and we are in a house
That is not ours, sitting at a table
Enjoying minutes of a rented silence,
The upstairs people gone. The pigeons lull
To sleep the under-tens and invalids,
The tree shakes out its shadows to the grass,
The roses rove through the wilds of my neglect.
Our lives flap, and we have no hope of better
Happiness than this, not much to show for love
Than how we are, or how this evening is,
Unpeopled, silent, and where we are alive
In a domestic love, seemingly alone.
All other lives worn down to trees and sunlight.
Looking forward to a visit from the cat.

Douglas Dunn

TABLE IN THE SUN
Detail
by Henri Le Sidaner

ANNABEL LEE

It was many and many a year ago,
   In a kingdom by the sea,
That a maiden there lived whom you may know
   By the name of Annabel Lee;
And this maiden she lived with no other thought
   Than to love and be loved by me.

***I* was a child and *she* was a child,**
   In this kingdom by the sea,
But we loved with a love that was more than love—
   I and my Annabel Lee—
With a love that the wingèd seraphs of Heaven
   Coveted her and me.

And this was the reason that, long ago,
   In this kingdom by the sea,
   A wind blew out of a cloud, chilling
   My beautiful Annabel Lee;
So that her highborn kinsmen came
And bore her away from me,
To shut her up in a sepulchre
In this kingdom by the sea.

The angels, not half so happy in Heaven,
   Went envying her and me—
Yes!—that was the reason (as all men know,
   In this kingdom by the sea)
That the wind came out of the cloud by night,
   Chilling and killing my Annabel Lee.

But our love it was stronger by far than the love
   Of those who were older than we—
   Of many far wiser than we—
And neither the angels in Heaven above
   Nor the demons down under the sea
Can ever dissever my soul from the soul
   Of the beautiful Annabel Lee;

For the moon never beams, without bringing me dreams
   Of the beautiful Annabel Lee;
And the stars never rise, but I feel the bright eyes
   Of the beautiful Annabel Lee;
And so, all the night-tide, I lie down by the side
Of my darling—my darling—my life and my bride,
   In her sepulchre there by the sea—
   In her tomb by the sounding sea.

Edgar Allan Poe

Landscape (Moonlight)

by Thomas Cole

When Granny

Song-bird shut dem mout' an lissen,
Church bell don't bother to ring,
All de little stream keep quiet
When mi Granny sing.

De sun up in de sky get jealous,
Him wish him got her style,
For de whole place full o' brightness
When mi Granny smile.
First a happy soun' jus' bubblin'
From her belly, low an' sof',
Den a thunderclap o' merriment
When mi Granny laugh.

De tree dem start to swing dem branch dem,
Puss an' dawg begin to prance,
Everyt'ing ketch de happy fever
When mi Granny dance.

Everybody look out fe Granny
Mek sure dat she satisfy,
For de whole worl' full o' sadness
When mi Granny cry.

Valerie Bloom

RED HOUSE
Detail
by Kazimir Malevich

THE STORY
OF THE STAR BRIDE

Once in the hot Summer weather, a lovely girl, named Feather Woman, was sleeping among the tall prairie grasses by the side of her lodge. She awoke just as the Morning Star was rising. As she gazed at its brightness, it seemed so beautiful that she loved it with all her heart. She roused her sister, who was sleeping beside her, and said: "Oh, sister, look at the Morning Star! I will never marry anybody except that Star!"

The sister laughed at her, and, getting up, ran into the camp, and told what Feather Woman had said, and the people all mocked and laughed. But Feather Woman paid no heed to their unkind words, but rose each day at dawn, and gazed on the Morning Star.

One morning early, as she went alone to the river, to fetch water for the lodge, she beheld a bright youth standing in the river-path.

"Feather Woman," said he, smiling, "I am Morning Star. I have seen you gazing upward, and am now come to carry you back with me to my dwelling."

At this Feather Woman trembled greatly. Then Morning
Star took from his head a rich yellow plume. He placed it in
her right hand, while in her other hand he put a branch of
Juniper. And he bade her close her eyes, and she did so.

When she opened her eyes, she was in the Sky Land,
standing in front of a shining lodge, and Morning Star was
by her side. This was the home of his parents, the Sun
and the Moon.

The Sun was away, casting his hottest Summer rays on the
parched Earth, but the Moon was at home, and she welcomed
Feather Woman kindly. She dressed the girl in a soft robe
of buckskin trimmed with Elk-teeth. And
when the Sun came back that night, he called
Feather Woman his daughter.

So she was married to Morning Star, and
they lived happily in the shining lodge. In
time they had a little son, whom they named
Star-Boy.

One day the Moon gave Feather Woman
a root-digger, and told her to go about
the Sky Land, and dig up all kinds of
roots; but on no account to touch the
Great Turnip that grew near the lodge.
For if she did so, unhappiness
would come to them all.

A White Camellia

by Georgia O'Keeffe

So day after day, Feather Woman went out and dug roots. She often saw the Great Turnip, but though she never touched it, her heart was filled with a desire to see what lay beneath it.

One day as she was wandering near the lodge, she was so overcome by curiosity, that she laid Star-Boy on the ground, and taking her root-digger, began to dig around the Great Turnip. But the digger fastened itself in the side of the Turnip, and she could not withdraw it. Just then two large Cranes flew over her head, and she called them to help her. They sang a magic song, and the Great Turnip was uprooted.

Then Feather Woman looked down through the hole where the Turnip had been, and, lo, far below she saw the camp of the Blackfeet, where she had lived. The smoke ascended from the lodges, and she could hear the laughter of the playing children, and the songs of the women at work. The sight filled her with homesickness, and she went back weeping to the shining lodge.

As she entered, Morning Star looked earnestly at her, and said, "Alas! Feather Woman, you have uprooted the Great Turnip!"

The Sun and the Moon, also, were troubled, when they knew she had been disobedient to their wishes; and they said that she must return at once to Earth. So Morning Star took Feather Woman sadly by the hand, and placing little Star-Boy upon her shoulder, led her to the Spider Man who lived in the Sky Land.

Then the Spider Man wove a web through the hole made by the Great Turnip, and let Feather Woman and her child down to the Earth. And her people saw her coming like a falling Star.

She was welcomed by her parents, and they loved little Star-Boy. And though after that Feather Woman always lived with her people, she was not happy; but longed to return to the Sky Land, and see Morning Star. But her longings were in vain, and soon her unhappy life was ended.

LADDER TO THE MOON
by Georgia O´Keeffe

AFTER APPLE-PICKING

My long two-pointed ladder's sticking through a tree
Toward heaven still,
And there's a barrel that I didn't fill
Beside it, and there may be two or three
Apples I didn't pick upon some bough.
But I am done with apple-picking now.
Essence of winter sleep is on the night,
The scent of apples: I am drowsing off.
I cannot rub the strangeness from my sight
I got from looking through a pane of glass
I skimmed this morning from the drinking trough
And held against the world of hoary grass.
It melted, and I let it fall and break.
But I was well
Upon my way to sleep before it fell,
And I could tell
What form my dreaming was about to take.
Magnified apples appear and disappear,
Stem end and blossom end,
And every fleck of russet showing clear.
My instep arch not only keeps the ache,
It keeps the pressure of a ladder-round.
I feel the ladder sway as the boughs bend.
And I keep hearing from the cellar bin
The rumbling sound
Of load on load of apples coming in.
For I have had too much
Of apple-picking: I am overtired
Of the great harvest I myself desired.
There were ten thousand thousand fruit to touch,
Cherish in hand, lift down, and not let fall.
For all
That struck the earth,
No matter if not bruised or spiked with stubble,
Went surely to the cider-apple heap
As of no worth.
One can see what will trouble
This sleep of mine, whatever sleep it is.
Were he not gone,
The woodchuck could say whether it's like his
Long sleep, as I describe its coming on,
Or just some human sleep.

Robert Frost

YELLOW COW
by Franz Marc

CUPID FALLEN

The wind blew little Cupid down last night,
who, in the dim nook of the park, with guile
bending his bow, would watch us with a smile,
and give us a long day of dream-delight.

Last night's winds blew him down. Ah! sad to see
the broken marble at the breath of dawn,
scattered, the artist's faint-seen name upon
the base, among the shadows of a tree.

Oh, it is sad, this empty base of stone,
and melancholy fancies enter in
and wander through my dream where deep chagrin
calls up a future fated and alone.

Oh, sad!—And you yourself, yes? feel the pain
of this drear picture, through your frivolous eye
toys with the gold-and-crimson butterfly
fluttering above the fragments in the lane.

Paul Verlaine

NOCTURNE IN THE PARC ROYAL, BRUSSELS
by William Degouve de Nuncques

THE TWO MOTHERS
Detail.
by Giovanni Segantini

Moonlit
Menagerie

MOON OVER LANDSCAPE

by Paula Modersohn-Becker

THE MOON

The moon has a face like the clock in the hall;
She shines on thieves on the garden wall,
On streets and fields and harbour quays,
And birdies asleep in the forks of the trees.

The squalling cat and the squeaking mouse,
The howling dog by the door of the house,
The bat that lies in bed at noon,
All love to be out by the light of the moon.

But all of the things that belong to the day
Cuddle to sleep to be out of her way;
And flowers and children close their eyes
Till up in the morning the sun shall arise.

Robert Louis Stevenson

FULL MOON AND LITTLE FRIEDA

A cool small evening shrunk to a dog bark and the clank of a bucket—
And you listening.
A spider's web, tense for the dew's touch.
A pail lifted, still and brimming—mirror
To tempt a first star to a tremor.

Cows are going home in the lane there, looping the hedges with their warm
wreaths of breath—
A dark river of blood, many boulders,
Balancing unspilled milk.
"Moon!" you cry suddenly, "Moon! Moon!"

**The moon has stepped back like an artist gazing amazed at a work
That points at him amazed.**

Ted Hughes

THE OWL

Downhill I came, hungry, and yet not starved;
Cold, yet had heat within me that was proof
Against the North wind; tired, yet so that rest
Had seemed the sweetest thing under a roof.

Then at the inn I had food, fire, and rest,
Knowing how hungry, cold, and tired was I.
All of the night was quite barred out except
An owl's cry, a most melancholy cry

Shaken out long and clear upon the hill,
No merry note, nor cause of merriment,
But one telling me plain what I escaped
And others could not, that night, as in I went.

And salted was my food, and my repose,
Salted and sobered, too, by the bird's voice
Speaking for all who lay under the stars,
Soldiers and poor, unable to rejoice.

Edward Thomas

A WISE OLD OWL

**A wise old owl lived in an oak
The more he saw the less he spoke
The less he spoke the more he heard.
Why can't we all be like that wise old bird?**

Anonymous

SMALL HORNED OWL
IN A PINE TREE

by Utagawa Hiroshige

Rats

You want to be a fat cat, want to do the deals?
Fix the odds, pull the birds, eat expensive meals
that someone else has paid for? Then listen here, my son,
you'll need to do some studying and find out how it's done.
Forget the university, you'll get no help from that—
you want the proper low-down? Then you've got to ask a rat.
Your rat has got the attitude. He understands the skill,
lines the job up nice and quiet, moves in for the kill.
He's good at business, naturally. His sharp-nailed little paws
are into every document, deleting any clause
that doesn't suit his purposes. He's got a lot of friends
and uses them with ruthless charm to further his own ends.
He has it off with all their wives, denies it with a smile.
Accused, he sues—and blow me down, he's made another pile.
And should we reap the whirlwind, boy, there's no need to despair.
Amid the rubble and the filth, the rat will still be there.

Alison Prince

THE DANCE OF THE RATS

by Ferdinand van Kessel

The Performing Bear

by Carl Spitzweg

SIMON SMITH AND THE AMAZING DANCING BEAR

I may go out tomorrow if I can borrow a coat to wear
Oh, I'd step out in style with my sincere smile and my dancing bear

Outrageous, alarming
Courageous, charming

Oh, who would think a boy and bear
Could be well accepted everywhere
It's just amazing how fair people can be

Seen at the nicest places where well-fed faces all stop to stare
Making the grandest entrance is Simon Smith and his dancing bear

They'll love us, won't they?
They feed us, don't they?

Oh, who would think a boy and bear
Could be well accepted everywhere
It's just amazing how fair people can be

Who needs money when you're funny?
The big attraction everywhere
Will be Simon Smith and his dancing bear
It's Simon Smith and the amazing dancing bear

Randy Newman

Dog around the Block

Dog around the block, sniff,
Hydrant sniffing, corner, grating,
Sniffing, always, starting forward,
Backward, dragging, sniffing backward,
Leash at taut, leash at dangle,
Leash in people's feet entangle—
Sniffing dog, apprised of smellings,
Love of life, and fronts of dwellings,
Meeting enemies,
Loving old acquaintance, sniff,
Sniffing hydrant for reminders,
Leg against the wall, raise,
Leaving grating, corner greeting,
Chance for meeting, sniff, meeting,
Meeting, telling, news of smelling,
Nose to tail, tail to nose,
Rigid, careful, pose,
Liking, partly liking, hating,
Then another hydrant, grating,
Leash at taut, leash at dangle,
Tangle, sniff, untangle,
Dog around the block, sniff.

E. B. White

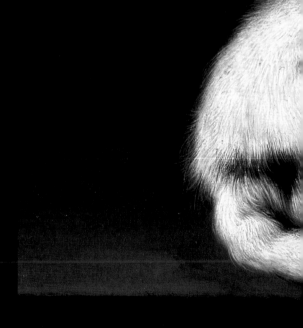

A SLEEPING DOG BESIDE A TERRA-
COTTA JUG, A BASKET, A PAIR OF CLOGS,
AND A PILE OF KINDLING WOOD
by Gerrit Dou

Carlito cannot sleep. He tosses back and forth in his hollow. Then back and forth again. He closes his eyes very tight and tries to snore. But that does not work when you are awake. And Carlito is very awake. Carlito then remembers, if you want to fall asleep, you have to count something. And preferably loud. Carlito looks around. What could he count then? Corn kernels are lying around next to the chicken coop. "One, two, three, four, five, six…"

Oops! What was that? Corn kernel number seven is gone. A chicken went past cackling, picked it up and swallowed it down.

Carlito is annoyed. "Of course, I cannot fall asleep without kernel number seven." He looks over to the chicken pen. The chickens are sitting on a pole and dozing off. "One, two, three, four, five…" counts Carlito.

The sixth chicken flutters down from the pole and climbs into its nest to lay an egg. Carlito scolds, "How dumb is that. I definitely cannot go to sleep without chicken number six." He goes to the chicken nests. Lots of eggs are lying there and waiting to be counted. Carlito starts immediately. "One, two, three, four…"

"Get out of there," someone snaps at him.

A family of martens has sneaked up to the nests. They stand with their front paws at the edge of the nests and each grabs an egg, then runs across the farmyard.

Carlito looks angrily at the martens. "One, two, three …"

"Look out!" shouts a marten and drops his egg.

The two farm cats, Pablo and Jinx, appear behind the chicken coop. The martens just about manage to escape through a hole in the fence.

"And what am I supposed to count now that the martens have gone?" asks an irritated Carlito. Pablo and Jinx do not care. They lie down and start to brush their fur. "One, two…" counts Carlito.

Suddenly, the cats jump up and run away at lightning speed. Carlito looks around him. It is Oskar the farm dog. He looks confused. "Where have the two cats gone?"

"Oh, dear," sighs Carlito. "Now I can only count Oskar."

"One," he says.

And then he fell asleep.

Karl Rühmann

DETAIL FROM THE GRABOW ALTARPIECE
by Master Bertram

FRAGMENT VI

Nightingale, herald of spring
With a voice of longing …

Sappho

A RED, RED ROSE

Oh my Luve's like a red, red rose
That's newly sprung in June:
Oh my Luve's like the melody
That's sweetly played in tune.

As fair art thou, my bonnie lass,
So deep in luve am I;
And I will luve thee still, my dear,
Till a' the seas gang dry.

Till a' the seas gang dry, my dear,
And the rocks melt wi' the sun:
And I will luve thee still, my dear,
While the sands o' life shall run.

And fare thee weel, my only Luve,
And fare thee weel a while!
And I will come again, my Luve,
Though it were ten thousand mile.

Robert Burns

NIGHTINGALE WITH ROSES
fragment of garden mural
from House of Golden Cupids in Pompeii

THE GOLDFISH

by Paul Klee

Huff

I AM in a tremendous huff—
Really, really bad.
It isn't any ordinary huff—
It's one of the best I've had.

I plan to keep it up for a month
Or maybe for a year
And you needn't think you can make me smile
Or talk to you. No fear.

I can do without you and her and them—
Too late to make amends.
I'll think deep thoughts on my own for a while,
Then find some better friends.

And they'll be wise and kind and good
And bright enough to see
That they should behave with proper respect
Towards somebody like me.

I do like being in a huff—
Cold fury is so heady.
I've been like this for half an hour
And it's cheered me up already.

Perhaps I'll give them another chance,
Now I'm feeling stronger,
But they'd better watch out—my next big huff
Could last much, much, much longer.

Wendy Cope

HOW THE POLAR BEAR MADE IT UP WITH THE ANIMALS

The polar bear was really angry when the sun disappeared. The skies overflowed with cold and darkness.

The white traveler became grouchy. One day he decided to climb down to earth and to get the sun.

"I have come to collect the sun," he said to the animals.

"We are not giving it to you," said the fox. He was trembling with fear. "Without the sun, there will be cold and darkness on the earth."

"But it's cold and dark in the heavens now," growled the polar bear.

The animals talked among themselves but did not reach an agreement. And then, Kurkyl, the raven, spoke up.

"Brothers and sisters, we all need the sun, even the polar bear. I suggest that the sun remain with us throughout the summer. The second half of the year, it should stay in the skies. It is wintertime then anyway and many animals hibernate at that time. That way it is fair."

And that is what they did. Since then, daytime in the Far East lasts a whole summer and nighttime all winter long. When the sun was in the heavens in winter, it was hibernating. Night did not need the sun. In summer, the sun was on earth. And the polar bear was always chasing after it.

Siberian fairy tale

Polar Bear Hunting

by Alexander Borisov

THE WILD SWANS AT COOLE

The trees are in their autumn beauty,
The woodland paths are dry,
Under the October twilight the water
Mirrors a still sky;
Upon the brimming water among the stones
Are nine-and-fifty swans.

The nineteenth autumn has come upon me
Since I first made my count;
I saw, before I had well finished,
All suddenly mount
And scatter wheeling in great broken rings
Upon their clamorous wings.

I have looked upon those brilliant creatures,
And now my heart is sore.
All's changed since I, hearing at twilight,
The first time on this shore,
The bell-beat of their wings above my head,
Trod with a lighter tread.

Unwearied still, lover by lover,
They paddle in the cold
Companionable streams or climb the air;
Their hearts have not grown old;
Passion or conquest, wander where they will,
Attend upon them still.

But now they drift on the still water,
Mysterious, beautiful;
Among what rushes will they build,
By what lake's edge or pool
Delight men's eyes when I awake some day
To find they have flown away?

William Butler Yeats

SWANS IN THE REEDS
by Caspar David Friedrich

THE HUNT IN THE FOREST

(also known as *The Hunt by Night* or *The Hunt*), *Detail*
by Paolo Uccello

Creepy, Crawlies and Things that Go Bump in the Night

HER KIND

I have gone out, a possessed witch,
haunting the black air, braver at night;
dreaming evil, I have done my hitch
over the plain houses, light by light:
lonely thing, twelve-fingered, out of mind.
A woman like that is not a woman, quite.
I have been her kind.

I have found the warm caves in the woods,
filled them with skillets, carvings, shelves,
closets, silks, innumerable goods;
fixed the suppers for the worms and the elves:
whining, rearranging the disaligned.
A woman like that is misunderstood.
I have been her kind.

I have ridden in your cart, driver,
waved my nude arms at villages going by,
learning the last bright routes, survivor
where your flames still bite my thigh
and my ribs crack where your wheels wind.
A woman like that is not ashamed to die.
I have been her kind.

Anne Sexton

WITCHES' SABBATH
by Francisco José de Goya

ANIMAL PICTURE WITH GENET

by Ludger Tom Ring the Younger

NATURE TRAIL

At the bottom of my garden
There's a hedgehog and a frog
And a lot of creepy-crawlies
Living underneath a log,
There's a baby daddy long legs
And an easy-going snail
And a family of woodlice,
All are on my nature trail.

There are caterpillars waiting
For their time to come to fly,
There are worms turning the earth over
As ladybirds fly by,
Birds will visit, cats will visit
But they always chose their time
And I've even seen a fox visit
This wild garden of mine.

Squirrels come to nick my nuts
And busy bees come buzzing
And when the night time comes
Sometimes some dragonflies come humming,
My garden mice are very shy
And I've seen bats that growl
And in my garden I have seen
A very wise old owl.

My garden is a lively place
There's always something happening,
There's this constant search for food
And then there's all that flowering,
When you have a garden
You will never be alone
And I believe we all deserve
A garden of our own.

Benjamin Zephaniah

BIRCH NOSE

ONE EVENING, grandpa said to grandma, "Bake me some biscuits. I have not hunted for a while and, tomorrow, I want to go into the forest."

"It's been a long time since you went hunting and there is no point anyway," muttered grandma. "Do you want the forest spirits to eat you?"

"Forest spirits here, forest spirits there! I am going anyway," answered grandpa. And he went to bed.

He got up in the morning and asked, "Did you make my biscuits?"

"No," answered grandma. "You are not going into the forest."

"I am!" said grandpa.

"You are not going!" said grandma.

And so they argued for half the day.

The sun was setting in the second half of the day when grandpa left the house. It was a long way to the hunting lodge, where he sometimes stayed for weeks on end as a youngster.

The sun sank, it became gloomy and then totally dark, but he still had not reached the lodge.

Grandma was probably right, he thought. The forest spirits will eat me up. It would have been better not to come!

He was so scared that his legs trembled.

But he carried on. I'll not be so afraid in the lodge, he thought. It's not that far now.

Then he saw light shimmering through the trees. He went closer. The light was coming from the window of the hunting lodge.

A huntsman must have arrived before me, thought grandpa. That's nice, we'll spend the night together.

Nonetheless, he did not go straight in, but peeked through the window.

Oh, what a horror! Sitting at the stove, were two, enormous forest spirits with bare, hairy arms and bare, hairy legs. One was skinning the fur from a red animal and the other was taking the fur off a black animal. Grandpa rocked back from the window and stood on the branch of a birch tree.

The branch broke with a loud snap!

"Oy!" shouted one of the forest spirits in a coarse voice.

"Heh," yelled the other.

Grandpa crept back to the window.

He peered and listened.

"Why are we so afraid?" asked the first forest spirit.

"I don't know," answered the second. "Is there anyone on earth stronger than we are?" He was trembling too.

"What was that?" asked the first forest spirit.

"Perhaps a tree branch cracked," answered the second.

"Oh, be quiet. My heart has stopped out of pure fright! Say again. What was that?"

"A tree branched snapped."

"Oh, be quiet! How can it break?" At the window, grandpa thought, I can see now who is more afraid. And we'll soon see which of us gets even more afraid! He carved off a piece of birch bark, curved it into a spout and stuck it on his nose. Now he had quite a big, long nose. He stuck his head through the window and shouted, "Birch nose is coming to visit! Woo-hoo-hoo-hoo!"

The forest spirits jumped up, knocked the door open and stormed off blindly into the night. The clatter of their feet rumbled through the dark forest.

Grandpa put the door back on, entered the lodge and went to sleep. Whether he actually went hunting is not known, but he brought home the pelt of the red animal and the pelt of the black animal, gave them to grandma and said, "And you did not want me to go into the forest!"

A fairy tale from the early Mansi hunting people of the Ural Mountains

BIRCH TREES IN THE EVENING
by Alexander Jakowlew Golowin

TO DO LIST

- Sharpen all pencils.
- Check off-side rear tyre pressure.
- Defrag hard drive.
- Consider life and times of Donald Campbell, CBE.
- Shampoo billiard-room carpet.
- Learn one new word per day.
- Make circumnavigation of Coniston Water by foot, visit Coniston Cemetery to pay respects.
- Achieve Grade 5 Piano by Easter.
- Go to fancy dress party as Donald Campbell complete with crash helmet and life jacket.
- Draft pro-forma apology letter during meditation session.
- Check world-ranking.
- Skim duckweed from ornamental pond.
- Make fewer "apples to apples" comparisons.
- Consider father's achievements only as barriers to be broken.
- Dredge Coniston Water for sections of wreckage/macabre souvenirs.
- Lobby service-provider to un-bundle local loop network.
- Remove all invasive species from British countryside.
- Build 1/25 scale model of Bluebird K7 from toothpicks and spent matches.
- Compare own personality with traits of those less successful but more popular.
- Eat (optional).
- Breathe (optional).
- Petition for high-speed fibre-optic broadband to this postcode.
- Order by express delivery DVD copy of Across the Lake starring Anthony Hopkins as "speed king Donald Campbell."
- Gain a pecuniary advantage.
- Initiate painstaking reconstruction of Donald Campbell's final seconds using archive film footage and forensic material not previously released into the public domain.
- Polyfilla all surfaces cracking to Bonneville Salt Flats, Utah.
- Levitate.
- Develop up to four thousand five hundred pounds/force of thrust.
- Carry on regardness despite suspected skull fracture.
- Attempt return run before allowing backwash ripples to completely subside.
- Open her up.
- Subscribe to convenient one-a-day formulation of omega oil capsules for balanced and healthy diet.
- Reserve full throttle for performance over "measured mile."
- Relocate to dynamic urban hub.
- Eat standing up to avoid time-consuming table manners and other non-essential mealtime rituals.
- Remain mindful of engine cutout caused by fuel-starvation.
- Exceed upper limits.
- Make extensive observations during timeless moments of somersaulting prior to impact.
- Disintegrate.

Simon Armitage

THE PRINCESS: SWEET AND LOW

Sweet and low, sweet and low,
Wind of the western sea,
Low, low, breathe and blow,
Wind of the western sea!
Over the rolling waters go,
Come from the dying moon, and blow,
Blow him again to me;
While my little one, while my pretty one, sleeps.

Sleep and rest, sleep and rest,
Father will come to thee soon;
Rest, rest, on mother's breast,
Father will come to thee soon;
Father will come to his babe in the nest,
Silver sails all out of the west,
Under the silver moon:
Sleep, my little one, sleep, my pretty one, sleep.

Alfred, Lord Tennyson

THE BIG MOON
by Marianne von Werefkin

SCAREDY-CATS

Bruno **cannot sleep.** Bruno does not want to sleep.

"One more story," he pleads.

"No," says Lisi. "I have read so many already. And in any case, I still have to learn French and draw a picture for Miss Kallisch."

Nonetheless, she still reads him a story.

Bruno, however, still cannot get to sleep. He doesn't want to sleep.

"Just one more st…" says Bruno, but before he can finish with "…ory," his big sister has already given him a kiss and pulled the thick blanket right up to his chin.

"You mustn't go out, Lisi," whines Bruno, and explains why: "Fear always comes at nighttime."

Lisi takes a good look around the room, even under the bed. There is no room under there, thinks Bruno, only the big box with the costumes in it.

"I cannot see anyone," Lisi says. "And I cannot hear or smell anything either."

Then she stands up and smiles at Bruno.

"If this fear should call out for you, I will send it to the Sea Cucumber," Lisi says as she leaves the room.

Sea Cucumber is what Bruno and Lisi call the neighbor who refuses to return their ball. The ball had only gone over the fence a couple of times by accident. Nonetheless, the Sea Cucumber became very green with anger and screamed furiously. Very scary!

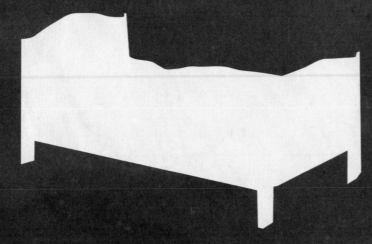

Bruno stares at the wall. Lisi has been going to school for so long now. Doesn't she know she can't send the fear to the Sea Cucumber? And she seems to need glasses. Can't she see what's happening? Can't she hear the faint squeaking? Does she have a cold? Doesn't she notice the moldy smell?

The fear has long been there. Even Bruno missed it because the stories were so funny. It must have crept in while Lisi was reading. Not through the door. No. The fear crept in through the walls.

And now it is crouching in the corner, by the wall where Bruno likes to build his knight's castle during the day. Now he can't move. He can only glare toward the fear. The fear glares right back at him. It is scratching at the plaster with its fingernails. Bruno knows that it will scratch him too.
That is why he has to keep his eyes pealed open so that it does not come out from the corner. With every blink, the fear could move a little bit more away from the wall. And crawl closer to his bed. Bruno continues to stare at the fear.

KNOCK … KNOCK, KNOCK. The sound is coming from above, from the skylight. It sounds as though a bony finger is tapping. Has the fear asked for a relative to come help? How can Bruno stare at two fears at the same time so that they do not move? His eyes cannot squint that far apart. **KNOCK, KNOCK.** That noise is back again. It does, however, sound like a bird pecking with its beak at the windowpane. Bruno just wants to take a quick look.

Thankfully, it is only the moon that is swinging back and forth in the middle of the pane like a silvery white penguin. The moon has known Bruno for a while now. It visits him every two weeks or so. But it has never knocked. Does it want to tell him something?

Bruno kicks off the covers and climbs on to the headboard of his bed. If he stretches far enough, he can push the window open enough to leave a small gap. Just far enough that the moon can whisper a secret to him … an unbelievable secret!

Bruno almost falls off the bed. "Are you sure?" asks the moon. The moon grins like someone very sure of himself.

The box is soon pulled out from under the bed. The moon helps Bruno choose something. The magician's costume with the midnight-blue cape and the pointed hat is just the thing.
Powerful and scary at the same time.

Bruno slips into the costume. Then he springs into the dark corner of the room, straight toward the fear. "BOOO!" he shouts, his arms in the air.
Again, as loud as he can, he shouts, "Boooo!!! **BOO! BOO!**"
The moon was not lying. The fear is trembling.
Now, Bruno's friend shines right into the furthest corner of the room. The fear has crept away. Bruno feels the wall with his fingers. There is no longer any trace of the fear.

Bruno tries to thank the moon, but it has already shuffled off. Only a glimpse of its white behind is visible. Bruno's eyes finally close.

"I am definitely sending the fear over to the Sea Cucumber," says Lisi on Tuesday evening, after reading Bruno seven stories in a row.

"No," says Bruno. "That would be mean. It would only get afraid. Didn't you know that poor old fear is a scaredy-cat?"

Annette Roeder

DARK GODS
by Max Ernst

GIPSY SONG

In the drizzling mist, with the snow high-pil'd,
In the Winter night, in the forest wild,
I heard the wolves with their ravenous howl,
I heard the screaming note of the owl:
Wille wau wau wau!
Wille wo wo wo!
Wito hu!

I shot, one day, a cat in a ditch—
The dear black cat of Anna the witch;
Upon me, at night, seven were-wolves came down,
Seven women they were, from out of the town.
Wille wau wau wau!
Wille wo wo wo!
Wito hu!

I knew them all; ay, I knew them straight;
First, Anna, then Ursula, Eve, and Kate,
And Barbara, Lizzy, and Bet as well;
And forming a ring, they began to yell:
Wille wau wau wau!
Wille wo wo wo!
Wito hu!

Then call'd I their names with angry threat:
"What wouldst thou, Anna? What wouldst thou, Bet?"
At hearing my voice, themselves they shook,
And howling and yelling, to flight they took.
Wille wau wau wau!
Wille wo wo wo!
Wito hu!

Johann Wolfgang von Goethe

THREE WOMEN AND
THREE WOLVES
by Eugène Samuel Grasset

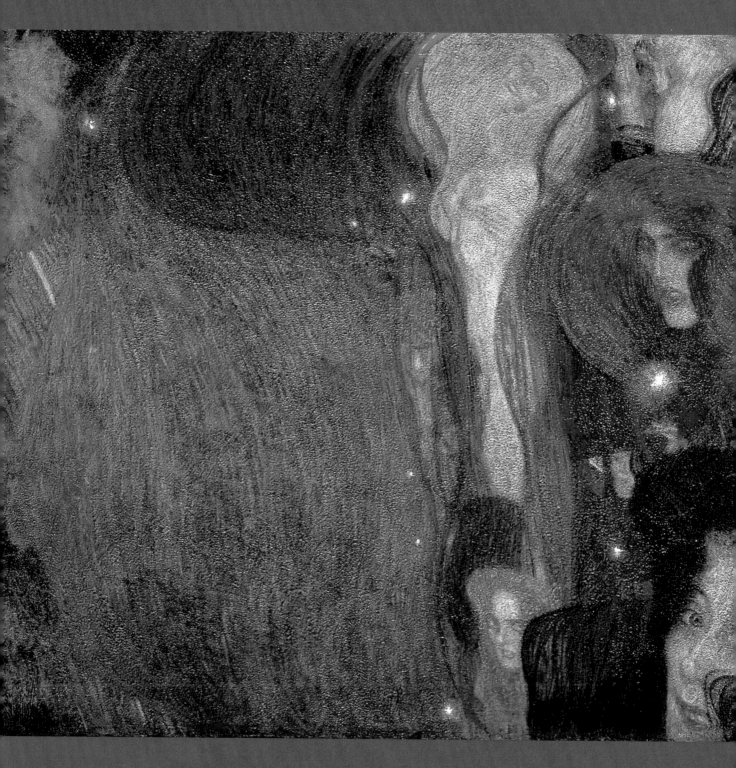

Irrlichter (Will-o'-the-Wisp)

by Gustav Klimt

The Will O' the Wisp

Where the snake lurks in the tangled grass,
By the slippery brink of the dank morass,
Merrily O! Merrily O!
I light my lamp, and forth I go!
And to lure astray the lated wight,
I shine all night in the swampy hollows,
Merrily O! Merrily O!
Wailing and woe to the fool who follows!

O! Love and Friendship and I make three,
We roam together in company!
Merrily O! Merrily O!
We light our lamps, and forth we go!
Friendship showeth a steady ray,
But its dupes ne'er dream that its heart is hollow,
Merrily O! Merrily O!
Wailing and woe to the fools who follow!

O! Love indeed hath a fairer gleam;
What is so bright as her first fond dream?
Merrily O! Merrily O!
We light our lamps, and forth we go!
An early blight if that love be true,
A broken heart if that love be hollow!
Merrily O! Merrily O!
Wailing and woe to the fools who follow!

Charles Mackay

LIFE DOESN'T FRIGHTEN ME

Shadows on the wall
Noises down the hall
Life doesn't frighten me at all

Bad dogs barking loud
Big ghosts in a cloud
Life doesn't frighten me at all

Mean old Mother Goose
Lions on the loose
They don't frighten me at all

Dragons breathing flame
On my counterpane
That doesn't frighten me at all.

I go boo
Make them shoo
I make fun
Way they run
I won't cry
So they fly
I just smile
They go wild

Life doesn't frighten me at all.

Tough guys fight
All alone at night
Life doesn't frighten me at all.

Panthers in the park
Strangers in the dark
No, they don't frighten me at all.

That new classroom where
Boys all pull my hair
(Kissy little girls
With their hair in curls)
They don't frighten me at all.

Don't show me frogs and snakes
And listen for my scream,
If I'm afraid at all
It's only in my dreams.

I've got a magic charm
That I keep up my sleeve
I can walk the ocean floor
And never have to breathe.

Life doesn't frighten me at all
Not at all
Not at all.

Life doesn't frighten me at all.

Maya Angelou

MOON AND FLOWERS

by Utagawa Hiroshige

... or a hot cup of tea

PERSIAN HERBAL FLOWER TEA

Ingredients for two people

1/5 cup of borage petals,
1/5 cup of valerian leaves
1 teaspoon of crushed dried lime
Sugar or honey to taste

Put the petal leaves into a teapot and
pour in boiling water. Add the lime
and brew for 30 minutes.
Sweeten according to taste.

The tea is particularly tasty when only the
flesh of the limes are used, not the peel.
To do this, break open the dried limes and
scrape out the inside!

CROSSING THE DESERT AT SUNSET
Detail
by Karl Friedrich Christian Welsch

Minds Ablaze

WHERE DO YOU GET YOUR IDEAS FROM?

From the **space** between my ears
from the **world** behind my eyes
from delving **deep inside** me
where **inspiration** lies
From **memories** that haunt me
from things I **hear** and **see**
from **mystical concoctions**
of **fact** and **fantasy**
   From **words** that come and find me
      from **dreaming** hard and long
         from **life** and **books** and music
           my **poems:** that's **where** they're from

James Carter

THE SLEEPING SHEPHERD

by Guy Pierre Fauconnet

Interior in Strandgade, Sunlight on the Floor

by Vilhelm Hammershoi

No. 115 Dreams

The living room remembers Gran dancing to Count Basie.
The kitchen can still hear my aunts fighting on Christmas day.
The hall is worried about the loose banister.
The small room is troubled by the missing hamster.
The toilet particularly dislikes my Grandfather.
The wallpaper covers up for the whole family.

And No. 115 dreams of lovely houses by the sea.
And No. 115 dreams of one night in the country.

The stairs are keeping schtum about the broken window.
The toilet's sick of the trapped pipes squealing so.
The walls aren't thick enough for all the screaming.
My parent's bedroom has a bed in a choppy sea.
My own bedroom loves the bones of me.
My brother's bedroom needs a different boy.

And No. 115 dreams of yellow light, an attic room.
And No. 115 dreams of a chimney, a new red roof.

And the red roof dreams of robin redbreasts
tap dancing on the red dance floor in the open air.

Jackie Kay

In Mrs Tilscher's Class

You could travel up the Blue Nile
with your finger, tracing the route
while Mrs Tilscher chanted the scenery.
Tana. Ethiopia. Khartoum. Aswân.
That for an hour, then a skittle of milk
and the chalky Pyramids rubbed into dust.
A window opened with a long pole.
The laugh of a bell swung by a running child.

This was better than home. Enthralling books.
The classroom glowed like a sweet shop.
Sugar paper. Coloured shapes. Brady and Hindley
faded, like the faint, uneasy smudge of a mistake.
Mrs Tilscher loved you. Some mornings, you found
she'd left a good gold star by your name.
The scent of a pencil slowly, carefully, shaved.
A xylophone's nonsense heard from another form.

Over the Easter term, the inky tadpoles changed
from commas into exclamation marks. Three frogs
hopped in the playground, freed by a dunce,
followed by a line of kids, jumping and croaking
away from the lunch queue. A rough boy
told you how you were born. You kicked him, but stared
at your parents, appalled, when you got back home.

That feverish July, the air tasted of electricity.
A tangible alarm made you always untidy, hot,
fractious under the heavy, sexy sky. You asked her
how you were born and Mrs Tilscher smiled,
then turned away. Reports were handed out.
You ran through the gates, impatient to be grown,
as the sky split open into a thunderstorm.

Carol Ann Duffy

Kairouan I
by August Macke

HUSH LITTLE BABY

Hush little ba - by, don't say a word,

Ma - ma's gonna buy you a Mock - ing - bird.

And if that mockingbird won't sing,
Mama's gonna buy you a diamond ring.

And if that diamond ring turns brass,
Mama's gonna buy you a looking glass.

And if that looking glass gets broke,
Mama's gonna buy you a billy goat.

And if that billy goat won't pull,
Mama's gonna buy you a cart and bull.

And if that cart and bull turn over,
Mama's gonna buy you a dog named Rover.

And if that dog named Rover won't bark,
Mama's gonna buy you a horse and a cart.

And if that horse and cart fall down,
You'll still be the sweetest little baby in town!

Traditional

THE POOR MAN'S STORE
by John Frederick Peto

THE END OF SUMMER

SWEET SMELL of phlox drifting across the lawn—
an early warning of the end of summer.
August is fading fast, and by September
the little purple flowers will all be gone.

Season, project, and vacation done.
One more year in everybody's life.
Add a notch to the old hunting knife
Time keeps testing with a horny thumb.

Over the summer months hung an unspoken
aura of urgency. In late July
galactic pulsings filled the midnight sky
like silent screaming, so that, strangely woken,

we looked at one another in the dark,
then at the milky magical debris
arcing across, dwarfing our meek mortality.
There were two ways to live: get on with work,

redeem the time, ignore the imminence
of cataclysm; or else take it slow,
be as tranquil as the neighbors' cow
we love to tickle through the barbed wire fence
(she paces through her days in massive innocence,
or, seeing green pastures, we imagine so).

In fact, not being cows, we have no choice.
Summer or winter, country, city, we
are prisoners from the start and automatically,
hemmed in, harangued by the one clamorous voice.

Not light but language shocks us out of sleep
ideas of doom transformed to meteors
we translate back to portents of the wars
looming above the nervous watch we keep.

Rachel Hadas

THE ENTIRE CITY

by Max Ernst

SLEIGH RIDE

by Ernst Ludwig Kirchner

THE ICE CART

Perched on my city office-stool,
I watched with envy, while a cool
And lucky carter handled ice …
And I was wandering in a trice,
Far from the grey and grimy heat
Of that intolerable street,
O'er sapphire berg and emerald floe,
Beneath the still, cold ruby glow
Of everlasting Polar night,
Bewildered by the queer half-light,
Until I stumbled, unawares,
Upon a creek where big white bears
Plunged headlong down with flourished
    heels
And floundered after shining seals
Through shivering seas of blinding blue.
And as I watched them, ere I knew,
I'd stripped, and I was swimming too,
Among the seal-pack, young and hale,
And thrusting on with threshing tail,
With twist and twirl and sudden leap
Through crackling ice and salty deep—

Diving and doubling with my kind,
Until, at last, we left behind
Those big, white, blundering bulks
    of death,
And lay, at length, with panting breath
Upon a far untravelled floe,
Beneath a gentle drift of snow—
Snow drifting gently, fine and white,
Out of the endless Polar night,
Falling and falling evermore
Upon that far untravelled shore,
Till I was buried fathoms deep
Beneath the cold white drifting sleep—
Sleep drifting deep,
Deep drifting sleep …

The carter cracked a sudden whip:
I clutched my stool with startled grip.
Awakening to the grimy heat
Of that intolerable street.

Wilfrid Gibson

119

Extract from Alice in Wonderland

The White Rabbit put on his spectacles.
"Where shall I begin, please your Majesty?" he asked.
"Begin at the beginning," the King said gravely,
"and go on till you come to the end: then stop."
These were the verses the White Rabbit read:—

"They told me you had been to her,
   And mentioned me to him:
She gave me a good character,
   But said I could not swim.

He sent them word I had not gone
   (We know it to be true):
If she should push the matter on,
   What would become of you?

I gave her one, they gave him two,
   You gave us three or more;
They all returned from him to you,
   Though they were mine before.

If I or she should chance to be
   Involved in this affair,
He trusts to you to set them free,
   Exactly as we were.

My notion was that you had been
   (Before she had this fit)
An obstacle that came between
   Him, and ourselves, and it.

Don't let him know she liked them best,
   For this must ever be
A secret, kept from all the rest,
   Between yourself and me."

"That's the most important piece
of evidence we've heard yet,"
said the King.

Lewis Carroll

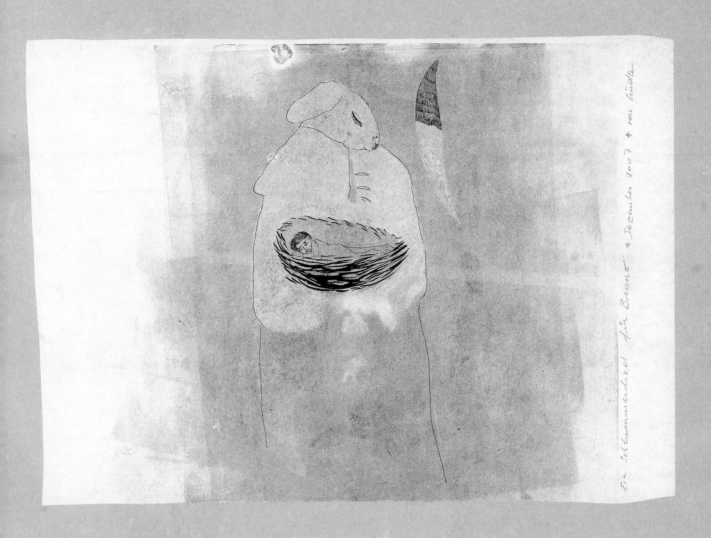

A Lullaby for Bruno

by Linda Wolfsgruber

HEAT

O wind, rend open the heat,
cut apart the heat,
rend it to tatters.

Fruit cannot drop
through this thick air—
fruit cannot fall into heat
that presses up and blunts
the points of pears
and rounds the grapes.

Cut the heat—
plough through it,
turning it on either side
of your path.

Hilda Doolittle

FURNACES AT COUILLET
by Maximilien Luce

CARNIVAL EVENING

A sense of peace and balance.
A pattern with a darkening sky.
Three disconnected clouds fly by
As if forgotten
By the glowering, snow filled ones
Rolling across the horizon.
Stark, leafless trees, wintered skeletons.
A kind of gazebo or summer house.

Upon the hilltop two figures,
Pierrot and his Columbine?
They are dressed as clowns.
Her arm is slipped in his
Trustingly; an old intimacy.
He, turning towards her
Solicitously, showing that he cares,
Seems to be about to speak.

Don't they feel cold, these lovers
As the moonlight picks them out?
Or are they too involved
To notice anything but each other?
Young lovers, yet forlorn,
Sad somehow,
Like victims of a secret love.
Delicate and fragile
They stand in the moonlight all alone.

Margery Rehman

CARNIVAL EVENING
by Henri Rousseau

IN THE MID-MIDWINTER

after John Donne's "A Nocturnal upon St. Lucy's Day"

AT **midday** on the year's midnight
into my mind came
I saw the new moon late yestreen
wi the auld moon in her airms
though, no,
there is no moon of course—
there's nothing very much of anything to speak of
in the sky except a gey dreich greyness
rain-laden over Glasgow and today
there is the very least of even this for us to get
but
the light comes back
the light always comes back
and this begins tomorrow with
however many minutes more of sun and serotonin.

Meanwhile
there will be the winter moon for us to love the longest,
fat in the frosty sky among the sharpest stars,
and lines of old songs we can't remember
why we know
or when first we heard them
will aye come back
once in a blue moon to us
unbidden

and bless us with their long-travelled light.

Liz Lochhead

NOCTURNE: BLUE AND SILVER – CHELSEA
by James Abbott McNeill Whistler

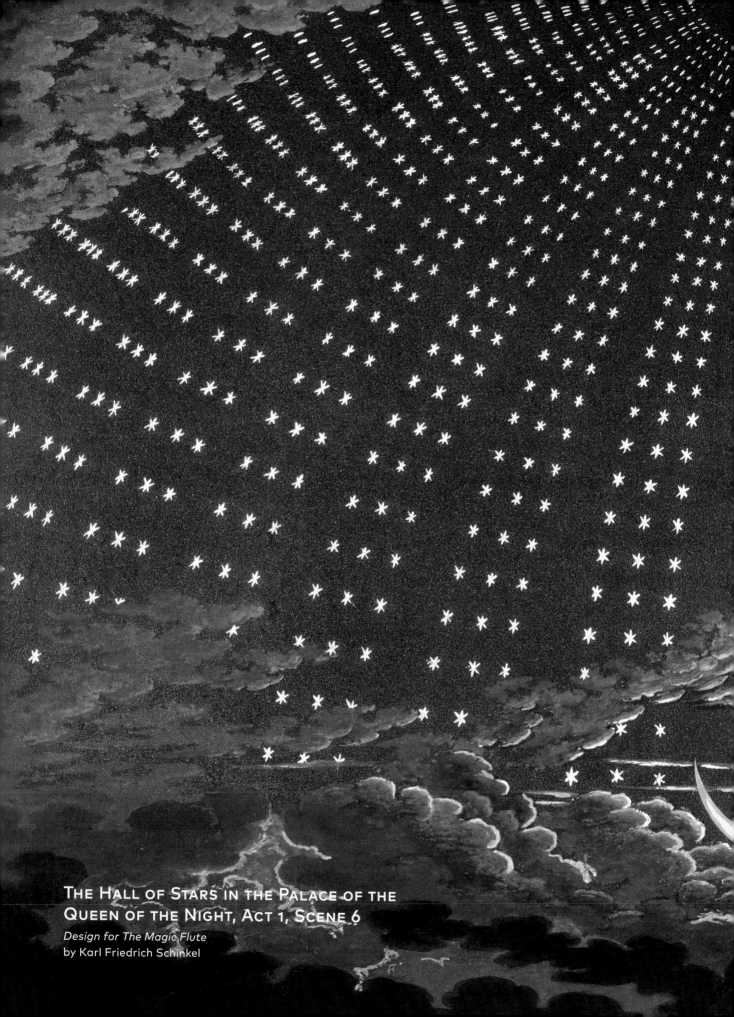

The Hall of Stars in the Palace of the Queen of the Night, Act 1, Scene 6

Design for The Magic Flute
by Karl Friedrich Schinkel

Midnight and Magic

I Am in Need of Music that Would Flow

I am in need of music that would flow
Over my fretful, feeling fingertips,
Over my bitter-tainted, trembling lips,
With melody, deep, clear, and liquid-slow.
Oh, for the healing swaying, old and low,
Of some song sung to rest the tired dead,
A song to fall like water on my head,
And over quivering limbs, dream flushed to glow!

There is a magic made by melody:
A spell of rest, and quiet breath, and cool
Heart, that sinks through fading colors deep
To the subaqueous stillness of the sea,
And floats forever in a moon-green pool,
Held in the arms of rhythm and of sleep.

Elizabeth Bishop

THREE PUTTI STANDING ATOP CLOUDS, GAZING DOWNWARD IN ADORATION
by Bernardino Luini

FROM FROST AT MIDNIGHT

The Frost performs its secret ministry,
Unhelped by any wind. The owlet's cry
Came loud—and hark, again! loud as before.
The inmates of my cottage, all at rest,
Have left me to that solitude, which suits
Abstruser musings: save that at my side
My cradled infant slumbers peacefully.
'Tis calm indeed! so calm, that it disturbs
And vexes meditation with its strange
And extreme silentness. Sea, hill, and wood,
This populous village! Sea, and hill, and wood,
With all the numberless goings-on of life,
Inaudible as dreams! the thin blue flame
Lies on my low-burnt fire, and quivers not;
Only that film, which fluttered on the grate,
Still flutters there, the sole unquiet thing.

Dear Babe, that sleepest cradled by my side,
Whose gentle breathings, heard in this deep calm,
Fill up the interspersèd vacancies
And momentary pauses of the thought!
My babe so beautiful! it thrills my heart
With tender gladness, thus to look at thee,
And think that thou shalt learn far other lore,
And in far other scenes! For I was reared
In the great city, pent 'mid cloisters dim,
And saw nought lovely but the sky and stars.
But *thou,* my babe! shalt wander like a breeze
By lakes and sandy shores, beneath the crags
Of ancient mountain, and beneath the clouds,
Which image in their bulk both lakes and shores
And mountain crags: so shalt thou see and hear
The lovely shapes and sounds intelligible
Of that eternal language, which thy God
Utters, who from eternity doth teach
Himself in all, and all things in himself.
Great universal Teacher! he shall mould
Thy spirit, and by giving make it ask.

Therefore all seasons shall be sweet to thee,
Whether the summer clothe the general earth
With greenness, or the redbreast sit and sing
Betwixt the tufts of snow on the bare branch
Of mossy apple-tree, while the night-thatch
Smokes in the sun-thaw; whether the eave-drops fall
Heard only in the trances of the blast,
Or if the secret ministry of frost
Shall hang them up in silent icicles,
Quietly shining to the quiet Moon.

Samuel Taylor Coleridge

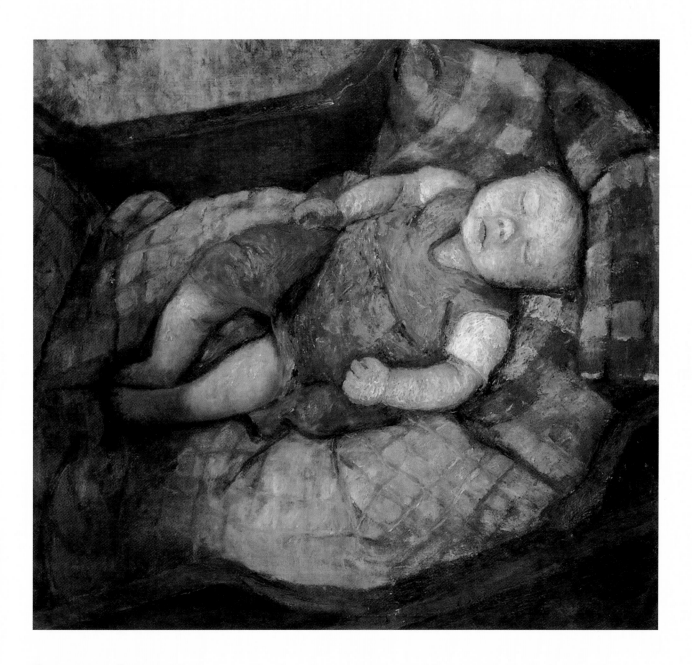

SLEEPING CHILD

by Paula Modersohn-Becker

LOVE AMONG THE RUINS

Where the quiet-coloured end of evening smiles,
    Miles and miles
On the solitary pastures where our sheep
    Half-asleep
Tinkle homeward thro' the twilight, stray or stop
    As they crop—
Was the site once of a city great and gay,
    (So they say)
Of our country's very capital, its prince
    Ages since
Held his court in, gathered councils, wielding far
    Peace or war.

Now the country does not even boast a tree,
    As you see,
To distinguish slopes of verdure, certain rills
    From the hills
Intersect and give a name to, (else they run
    Into one)
Where the domed and daring palace shot its spires
    Up like fires
O'er the hundred-gated circuit of a wall
    Bounding all
Made of marble, men might march on nor be prest
    Twelve abreast.

And such plenty and perfection, see, of grass
    Never was!
Such a carpet as, this summer-time, o'er-spreads
    And embeds
Every vestige of the city, guessed alone,
    Stock or stone—
Where a multitude of men breathed joy and woe
    Long ago;
Lust of glory pricked their hearts up, dread of shame
    Struck them tame;
And that glory and that shame alike, the gold
    Bought and sold.

Now—the single little turret that remains
    On the plains,
By the caper overrooted, by the gourd
    Overscored,
While the patching houseleek's head of blossom winks
    Through the chinks—
Marks the basement whence a tower in ancient time
    Sprang sublime,
And a burning ring, all round, the chariots traced
    As they raced,
And the monarch and his minions and his dames
    Viewed the games.

And I know, while thus the quiet-coloured eve
    Smiles to leave
To their folding, all our many-tinkling fleece
    In such peace,
And the slopes and rills in undistinguished grey
    Melt away—
That a girl with eager eyes and yellow hair
    Waits me there
In the turret whence the charioteers caught soul
    For the goal,
When the king looked, where she looks now, breathless, dumb
    Till I come.

ROMAN COUNTRYSIDE BY MOONLIGHT
by Anonymous

But he looked upon the city, every side,
    Far and wide,
All the mountains topped with temples, all the glades'
    Colonnades,
All the causeys, bridges, aqueducts,—and then
    All the men!
When I do come, she will speak not, she will stand,
    Either hand
On my shoulder, give her eyes the first embrace
    Of my face,
Ere we rush, ere we extinguish sight and speech
    Each on each.

In one year they sent a million fighters forth
    South and North,
And they built their gods a brazen pillar high
    As the sky
Yet reserved a thousand chariots in full force—
    Gold, of course.
O heart! oh blood that freezes, blood that burns!
    Earth's returns
For whole centuries of folly, noise and sin!
    Shut them in,
With their triumphs and their glories and the rest!
    Love is best.

Robert Browning

DETAIL OF CEILING FRESCO FROM AMBRAS CASTLE

by Giovanni Battista Fontana

A MENAGERIE OF ANIMALS

i.
Great grey belly porker,
toothy yawning slug,
cow-nosed submarine,
giant in the mud.
Unlikely ballerina
tip-toes underwater,
sleepy swampland-island,
river's favourite daughter.

ii.
Stripy-armoured tiny tiger,
pollen-pouched and humble,
a fairy-small furry flyer,
content to simply bumble.

iii.
An African agitator,
sleeping now, snapping later.
Living log with beady eyes,
a flash of jaws and something dies.

Antelope and sleek gazelle
know the dangers very well,
are careful by the river Nile's
toothy and serrated smiles.

iv.
Fish-chasing waiters,
waddling torpedoes,
ice-footed flipper-flappers,
swimmers with no speedos.

v.
Knitting hunter,
insect hater—
catch them now,
eat them later.

vi.
Orange as a sunset,
red as a pillar-box.
Entering the chicken coop,
unwelcome as Goldilocks.

vii.
As big as houses end to end,
glimpsed and then it's gone,
an island for a mariner
he won't step foot upon.

A water feature fountaining
between the foaming waves,
an oily mountain sinking fast,
takes plankton to their graves.

viii.
Purr-bearer,
fur-wearer,
tail-tosser,
mouse-bosser.

ix.
At first a dot,
then a hop.

A. F. Harrold

In the Old Age of the Soul

I do not choose to dream; there cometh on me
Some strange old lust for deeds.
As to the nerveless hand of some old warrior
The sword-hilt or the war-worn wonted helmet
Brings momentary life and long-fled cunning,
So to my soul grown old—
Grown old with many a jousting, many a foray,
Grown old with many a hither-coming and hence-going—
Till now they send him dreams and no more deed;
So doth he flame again with might for action,
Forgetful of the council of elders,
Forgetful that who rules doth no more battle,
Forgetful that such might no more cleaves to him
So doth he flame again toward valiant doing.

Ezra Pound

THE NIGHT
by Alexej von Jawlensky

THE FLIGHT INTO EGYPT
by Adam Elsheimer

THE MOTHER MOON

The moon upon the wide sea
Placidly looks down,
Smiling with her mild face,
Though the ocean frown.
Clouds may dim her brightness,
But soon they pass away,
And she shines out, unaltered,
O'er the little waves at play.
So 'mid the storm or sunshine,
Wherever she may go,
Led on by her hidden power
The wild sea must plow.

As the tranquil evening moon
Looks on that restless sea,
So a mother's gentle face,
Little child, is watching thee.
Then banish every tempest,
Chase all your clouds away,
That smoothly and brightly
Your quiet heart may play.
Let cheerful looks and actions
Like shining ripples flow,
Following the mother's voice,
Singing as they go.

Louisa May Alcott

ALL SILVER

THE LITTLE WATER SPRITE was captivated. He could not take his eyes away from the dancing women of the mist. Like drifting clouds, they took on shape after shape. They came together and parted before his very eyes. And it sometimes came about that one or another of them would melt away like smoke in the wind in the middle of all this beautiful floating flurry.

The little water sprite followed this fleeting hustle and bustle with such fascination that he failed to notice how a pale, reddish ray of light was rising up in the skies behind the hills. He only became aware of it when his father stopped playing the harp and gently called him.

"Look over there," shouted the water sprite's father in half voice and pointed to the shimmering spot on the edge of the sky. "He'll rise soon."

"Who will?" asked the water sprite in a similar mellow tone. However, as his father had started playing his harp again right at that moment, the boy swallowed back his question and thought: I am going to find out what he meant. The shimmering stripe on the edge of the skies was getting brighter and brighter, so the little water sprite looked on, tense with anticipation. The reddish glow rose higher and higher, flowing vigorously. Soon, the little sprite could see every single tree on the hills in front of him. Their trunks and treetops stood out so clearly in the silhouette against the glowing background. Then, all of a sudden, a radiant, circular disc appeared in the sky, golden yellow and glistening like an enormous marigold.

The water sprite boy could not hold back and shouted, "Father, it's the sun … !"

The sprite's father chuckled when he heard this and, without stopping to pluck his strings, replied: "But, boy. That is the moon rising."

"The … moon?"

"Yes, the moon," said the sprite's father. However, because he realized the boy could not really understand what that word meant, he went on to tell him about the moon: how it moves across the sky on clear nights; how it gets smaller and larger; how it sometimes disappears completely, yet always returns, growing full again; and about all that it has seen on its travels and all that it is yet to see, until the end of time. And every time he told the boy a part of the story, he played his harp, before speaking again. In the meantime, the moon had risen even higher. It gently swam into the heavens. The little water sprite had stretched back on the grass to get a better view of it.

Almost imperceptibly, the moon had changed its color. It had transformed from a marigold into a shining silver coin. And everything it touched with its rays took on a silver sheen. It had given a silver coating to the sky, the meadows, the pond, the reeds and the dancing women of the mist, as well as to the boat lying at the bank and the leaves on the trees.

"Now, it is heading straight for the old pasture," said the water sprite boy abruptly. "It will not get caught up in its branches, will it?"

"You can climb up over there," said the father, "and help it get over them."

"Yes," said the water sprite boy, "I'll do that."

And he quickly climbed up the old willow tree to lift the moon out of the branches. However, he had been worrying for no reason, for as much as he stretched and pushed himself, he could not reach the moon.

His father was just about to call him down, when he heard the boy ask in astonishment: "Do we also have a moon down in the pond?"

"Not that I know of," said the water sprite's father. "How would the moon get into the pond?"

"But I can see it," called the boy. "I can see them both! One in the sky and one down in the water. How nice it is to have a moon as well! As long as it does not swim away from us … But, you know what! I will catch it. If I jump down, I can get hold of it! Just think how mother will be surprised when I suddenly place the moon on our kitchen table for her!"

Before the father could make a reply to what he had heard (and it is possible that he was not projecting that), the water sprite boy rushed down from the willow and into the pond. As he fell, he stretched out his hands so that he would not miss the moon, which was floating and shining on the water.

But what was this?

As he touched the surface of the water with his fingertips, the moon broke up into rings of silver waves.

"Did you get it," asked the water sprite's father, the moment the spluttering boy had surfaced. However, he did not even wait for an answer because he saw that the boy was swimming in the middle of liquid silver and how silver drops sprayed from the boy's hair as he shook his head. And this made the water sprite father so pleased that he reached for his harp and did not stop playing for as long as the little sprite boy was taking his silvery bath down in the moonlit pond.

From The Little Water Sprite *by Otfried Preussler*

NEXT MARKET DAY

A maid goin' to Comber, her markets to larn,
To sell for her Mammy three hanks o' fine yarn.
She met with a young man along the highway
Which caused this young damsel to dally and stray.

Sit ye beside me, I mean ye no harm.
Sit ye beside me this new tune to larn.
Here is three guineas your Mammy to pay,
If you lay down your yarn till the next market day.

They sat down together, and the grass it was green.
The day was the fairest that ever was seen.
Oh the look in your eye beats a mornin' o' May,
I could sit by your side till the next market day.

The maid then went home and the words that he said,
And the air that he played her still rang in her head.
She says, I'll go find him by land or by sea
Till he learns me that tune called The Next Market Day.

Traditional

CARNIVAL AT NIGHT
by Ferdinand du Puigaudeau

Secret of the Stars

It was a beautiful, starry night and a little boy and his grandpa were walking through a field. The youngster was happy to be out with his grandpa. He was so good at telling stories and it seemed his grandpa picked out stories like other people pick flowers.

They stopped and looked up at the sky. "Isn't that wonderful?" said grandpa. "As if the stars were winking secret messages to us, don't you think?" "Yes!" said the boy, overawed. They both blew a few tiny clouds of air toward the sky, which shifted in the soft breeze. "Smoke signals," they grinned.

They came to a small pond. The starry sky was reflected in the rippling water, making it look as if the stars were rolling back and forth in high spirits. "Grandpa," said the boy all of a sudden. "Where do the stars actually come from? Can you tell me?"

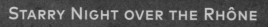

STARRY NIGHT OVER THE RHÔNE
by Vincent van Gogh

"Of course," said grandpa. "I know a story or two about that. For example, the one about the pirate."
"Oh, yes! I want to hear that one!" shouted the little boy.

And the grandpa explained: "A long, long time ago, there was a daring and feared pirate. He attacked large trading ships and stole their jewels and pearls, silver and gold. He was very skillful and brave. However, he became greedier and greedier. He wanted a huge sack of gold coins brought to his hiding place. But the sack was so full that it burst and the coins rolled all over the sky. And there, they still glisten and shine."
"Oh, so these are all gold coins. Amazing," marveled the boy.

"Well, maybe it was something different," grinned grandpa. And then he explained, "There was once a great magician. He could perform such magic that he became known every-where—here, there and truly everywhere. Then one night, out of boredom, he created a magical hat, glittering with stones, but then dozed off. Next, a mischievous bat tickled his nose. The magician woke up from his slumber, grabbed his hat, and—goodness—put it on his head. All of the stones fell out and were scattered right throughout the sky. And they are still sparkling and shining there to this day."
The little boy laughed. "I am sure the wizard was annoyed!"

But grandpa knew yet another story. "I once heard that the sky is the bottom of a huge cooking pot. Just imagine. Light is cooked in it the whole day long. The light, however, needs to be stirred all the time so that it does not burn. Over time, the base of the pot became very thin and full of holes through the constant stirring. There you have it: stars are simply the light shining through the tiny holes."

The little boy was delighted. He looked up to the sky and imagined there was someone up there swinging a giant cooking spoon.

"So," he thought, "the moon is also a hole in the bottom of the pot, just a much bigger one!"

Next, grandpa picked up the boy so that he could be even closer to the stars. "They were all just stories," he whispered in his ear. "Now, I will tell you the secret of the stars…"
The boy listened carefully.
"Every star you see is a child's wish. Every time, a child makes a firm wish for something very beautiful, a star appears in the heavens. And it stays there until the right time comes. Every time you look up to the skies, you should think about your wishes that are up there. The stars are a sign that you should never give up on those wishes. One day they will come true. And then a shooting star will fall from the sky."
"That's nice," whispered the little boy. "Grandpa, may I make a wish now?"
"Yes," nodded grandpa, "the more wishes, the brighter the skies become."

Then, the boy put his cheek on his grandpa's face and they both wished for something especially beautiful … and together their eyes searched for the new star.

Karl Rühmann

TOMORROW HAS YOUR NAME ON IT

Tomorrow has your name on it
It's written up there in the sky
As you set out on a journey
in search of the How? and the Why?

Oh the people you'll meet
The bright and the mad
The sights to be seen
The fun to be had.

Oh the dreams that you'll dream
The chances you'll take
The prizes you'll win
The hands that you'll shake.

But don't let your dreams
Get too big for their boots
Don't hanker after the flimflam of fame
If you hunger for mere celebrity
You'll be drawn like a moth to the flame.

For having dreams is not enough;
You must get down and do your stuff.
Take the ready with the rough.
Ride the punches, and my hunch is
You'll succeed when life gets tough.

And it will!
(That's also written in the sky
In a cobwebby corner of the Milky Way
A squillion zillion miles away)

Bullies will want to bully you
For that's what bullies do
And you'll feel small and miserable
(Don't worry, I would too).

Even Big Bad Wolves have nightmares,
One of the reasons they howl at the moon.
Being scared is Nature's medicine.
Not nice, but it's over soon.

There'll be days you're made to feel foolish
When your head seems made out of wood
When you blush, mumble and shuffle
Feel embarrassed and misunderstood.

Things will get lost or stolen
Life doesn't turn out as you'd planned
You get sick and then you get better—
What's gone wrong? You can't understand.

Take your time.
Sing your own songs and laugh out loud.
Weep if you need to
But away from the crowd.

Disappointments will ebb and flow
Like the tide upon the shore
But an angry storm will quickly go
And the sun rise up once more.

Oh the dreams that you'll dream
The promises you'll make
The friends that you find
Whom you'll never forsake.

Oh the dreams that you'll dream,
May the good ones come true.
Being young is an adventure
How I wish I were you.

Today is the tomorrow we worried about
Yesterday and all last night.
And as days go, as days they do.
It seemed to go all right.

So dream your dreams and journey
Be tomorrow foul or fine
So you can say at the end of it
"Amazing! Today was mine."

Roger McGough

IN BED

by Federico Zandomeneghi

SPIRIT OF THE NIGHT

by John Atkinson Grimshaw

Lists and Notes from
the English Editors

List of Artworks

George Dunlop Leslie (1835–1921). ALICE IN WONDERLAND, Brighton & Hove Museum & Art Galleries, Brighton, England. Photo: The Bridgeman Art Library, p. 8.

Jean Étienne Liotard (1702–1789). THE CHOCOLATE GIRL, c. 1743–44. Old Masters Picture Gallery, Dresden, Germany, p. 22.

Maximilien Luce (1858–1941). CAMARET, MOONLIGHT AND FISHING BOATS, 1894. Saint Louis Art Museum. Photo: Artothek, frontispiece.
FURNACES AT COUILLET, 1903. Private collection. Photo: Christie's Images Ltd – Artothek, p. 122.

Bernardino Luini, Successors (early 16th century): THREE PUTTI STANDING ATOP CLOUDS, GAZING DOWNWARD IN ADORATION, early 16th century. Private collection. Photo: Christie's Images Ltd – Artothek, p. 131.

August Macke (1887–1914). KAIROUAN I, 1914. Pinakothek der Moderne, Munich, Germany. Photo: Blauel Gnamm – Artothek, p. 113.

Kazimir Malevich (1879–1935). RED HOUSE, 1932. The State Russian Museum, St. Petersburg, Russia. Photo: Artothek, p. 49.

Édouard Manet (1832–1883). MOONLIGHT AT THE PORT OF BOULOGNE, 1868. Musée d'Orsay, Paris, France. Photo: Peter Willi – Artothek, p. 26.

Franz Marc (1880–1916). YELLOW COW, 1911. Lenbachhaus, Munich, Germany, p. 57.

Paula Modersohn-Becker (1876–1907). MOON OVER LANDSCAPE, c. 1900. Paula Modersohn-Becker Stiftung, Bremen, Germany, p. 62.
SLEEPING CHILD, 1904, Paula Modersohn-Becker Stiftung, Bremen, Germany, p. 133.

Claude Monet (1840–1926). THE HOUSES OF PARLIAMENT (EFFECT OF FOG), 1903–04. National Gallery of Art, Washington, DC, p. 17.
WATER LILIES, 1915. Neue Pinakothek, Munich, Germany. Photo: Blauel/Gnamm – Artothek, p. 14.

Ferdinand von Kessel (1648–1696) attributed: THE DANCE OF THE RATS, c. 1690. Städel Museum, Frankfurt am Main, Germany. Photo: U. Edelmann – Städel Museum – Artothek, p. 67.

Georgia O'Keeffe (1887–1986). LADDER TO THE MOON, 1958. Whitney Museum of American Art, New York, p. 55.
A WHITE CAMELLIA, 1938. Private collection, p. 52.

John Frederick Peto (1854–1907). THE POOR MAN'S STORE, 1885. Museum of Fine Arts, Boston, MA, USA, p. 115.

Ferdinand du Puigaudeau (1864–1930). CARNIVAL AT NIGHT, 1898. Photo: Artothek, p. 145.

Ludger Tom Ring the Younger (1522–1584). ANIMAL PICTURE WITH GENET, c. 1560. Westphalian State Museum of Art and Cultural History, Münster, Germany. Photo: LWL-LMKuK – Artothek, p. 86.

Henri Rousseau (1844–1910). CARNIVAL EVENING, 1886. Philadelphia Museum of Art, PA, USA. Photo: The Bridgeman Art Library, Cover/ p. 125.
THE DREAM, 1910. Museum of Modern Art, New York. Photo: Joseph S. Martin – Artothek, p. 40.

John Singer Sargent (1856–1925). CARNATION, LILY, LILY, ROSE, 1885–86. Tate Britain, London, p. 13.

Karl Friedrich Schinkel (1781–1841). THE HALL OF STARS IN THE PALACE OF THE QUEEN OF THE NIGHT, ACT 1, SCENE 6, Design for Mozart's *Magic Flute*, 1815. Deutsches Theatermuseum, Berlin, Germany. Photo: The Bridgeman Art Library, p. 128-129.

Giovanni Segantini (1858–1899). THE TWO MOTHERS, 1889. Private collection. Photo: Christie's Images Ltd – Artothek, p. 60-61.

Henri Le Sidaner (1862–1939). SPRING EVENING, 1935. Musée d'Arts de Nantes, France. Photo: The Bridgeman Art Library, p. 18.
TABLE IN THE SUN, 1924. Private collection. Photo: Christie's Images Ltd – Artothek , p. 45.

Carl Spitzweg (1808–1885). THE PERFORMING BEAR, c. 1868. Private collection. Photo: Artothek, p. 68.

Bernardo Strozzi (1581–1644). SLEEPING CHILD, date unknown. Residenzgalerie, Salzburg, Austria. Photo: Jochen Remmer – Artothek, p. 35.

Paolo Uccello (1397–1475). THE HUNT IN THE FOREST, c. 1460. Ashmolean Museum of Art and Archaeology, Oxford, England, p. 82-83.

Karl Friedrich Christian Welsch (1828–1904). CROSSING THE DESERT AT SUNSET, 1879. Private collection. Photo: Christie's Images Ltd – Artothek, p. 106-107.

Marianne von Werefkin (1860–1938). THE BIG MOON, 1923. Marianne Werefkin Foundation, Ascona, Switzerland, p. 94.

James Abbott McNeill Whistler (1834–1903). NOCTURNE: BLUE AND SILVER - CHELSEA, 1871. Tate Gallery, London. Photo: akg-images / Erich Lessing, p. 126.

Linda Wolfsgruber (1961–). A LULLABY FOR BRUNO, date unknown. Private collection, p. 121.

Federico Zandomeneghi (1841–1917). IN BED, 1874. Palazzo Pitti, Florence, Italy. Photo: Alinari – Artothek, p. 151.

LIST OF TEXTS AND POEMS

Louisa May Alcott (1832–1888). **THE MOTHER MOON,** 1856, p. 141.

William Allingham (1824–1889). **THE FAIRIES,** 1883, p. 42.

Maya Angelou (1928–2014). **LIFE DOESN'T FRIGHTEN ME.** In *Life Doesn't Frighten Me,* edited by Sara Jane Boyers (New York, US: Stewart, Tabori & Chang Inc, 1993), p. 104.

Anonymous. **A WISE OLD OWL,** p. 64.

Anonymous. **BIRCH NOSE,** p. 88.

Anonymous. **HOW THE POLAR BEAR MADE IT UP WITH THE ANIMALS,** p. 78.

Anonymous. **HUSH LITTLE BABY,** date unknown, p. 114.

Anonymous. **NEXT MARKET DAY,** As sung by Fiona Blackburn on her CD *Land of Passages,* p. 144.

Anonymous. **REMINISCENCES OF EARLY LIFE.** Extract from *The Graves of the Indians and Other Poems* (Boston, US: Hilliard, Gray, Little and Wilkins, 1827), p. 38.

Anonymous. **THE STORY OF THE STAR BRIDE.** In *The Red Indian Fairy Book,* by Frances Jenkins Olcott (1917), p. 50.

Simon Armitage (1963–). **TO DO LIST.** In *The Unaccompanied* (London, UK: Faber, Copyright © Simon Armitage, 2017), p. 92.

Laurence Binyon (1869–1943). **THE LITTLE DANCER.** In *The Oxford Book of Victorian Verse,* ed. by Arthur Quiller-Couch (Oxford, US: The Clarendon Press, 1922), p. 16.

Elizabeth Bishop (1911–1979). **I AM IN NEED OF MUSIC THAT WOULD FLOW.** In *The Complete Poems: 1927–1979* (New York, US: Farrar Straus Giroux, 1983), p. 130.

Valerie Bloom (1956–). **WHEN GRANNY.** 2000. In *Give the Ball to the Poet: A New Anthology of Caribbean Poetry,* edited by Georgie Horrell, Aisha Spencer, and Morag Styles (London, UK: Commonwealth Education Trust, 2014), p. 48.

Robert Browning (1812–1889). **LOVE AMONG THE RUINS,** In *Men and Women* (Boston, US: Ticknor & Fields, 1855), p. 134.

Robert Burns (1759–1796). **A RED, RED ROSE,** 1794, p. 74.

James Carter (1939–). **THE REALLYREALLYREALLY TRULYTRUETRUTH ABOUT... TEDDY BEARS.** In *Journey to the Centre of My Brain* (London, UK: Macmillan Children's Books, 2012), p. 24; **WHERE DO YOU GET YOUR IDEAS FROM?** (London, UK: Macmillan Children's Books, 2012), p. 108.

Lewis Carroll (1832–1898). Extract from *Alice in Wonderland,* 1865, p. 120.

Samuel Taylor Coleridge (1772–1834). **FROST AT MIDNIGHT,** 1798, p. 132.

Wendy Cope (1945–). **HUFF.** In *Don't be Scared: An Anthology for Children by Well-Loved Authors and Artists* (Bristol, UK: Redcliffe Press, 2016), p. 77.

Thomas Dekker (1572–1632). **GOLDEN SLUMBERS,** 1603, p. 28.

Hilda Doolittle (1886–1961). **HEAT,** 1916, p. 123.

Carol Ann Duffy (1955–). **IN MRS TILSCHER'S CLASS.** In *The Other Country* (London, UK: Carcanet Press, 2004), p. 112.

Douglas Dunn (1942–). **MODERN LOVE.** In *Selected Poems: 1964–1983* (London, UK: Faber & Faber, 1987), p. 44.

T. S. Eliot (1888–1965). **PRELUDES I,** 1910–117. In *Prufrock and Other Observations* (London, UK: Egoist Press), p. 16.

Robert Frost (1874–1963). **AFTER APPLE-PICKING,** 1914, p. 56.

Wilfrid Gibson (1878–1962). **THE ICE CART,** p. 119.

Johann Wolfgang von Goethe (1749–1832). **GIPSY SONG,** 1772, p. 100.

Rachel Hadas (1948–). **THE END OF SUMMER.** In *Halfway Down the Hall: New and Selected Poems* (Connecticut, US: Wesleyan University Press, 1998), p. 116.

A. F. Harrold (1975–). **A MENAGERIE OF ANIMALS.** In *Things You Find in a Poet's Beard* (Bristol, UK: Burning Eye Books, © A. F. Harrold, first published in *I Eat Squirrels* (Quirkstandard's Alternative, 2009), reproduced by kind permission of the author, p. 137.

Nathaniel Hawthorne (1804–1864). **THE OCEAN,** 1833, p. 15.

Robert Herrick (1591–1674). **DREAMS,** p. 15.

Ted Hughes (1930–1998). **FULL MOON AND LITTLE FRIEDA,** In *Wodwo* (London, UK: Faber & Faber, 1967), p. 63.

Heinz Janisch (1960–). **GOOD NIGHT! GOOD NIGHT!,** p. 30.

Jackie Kay (1961–). **NO. 115 DREAMS.** In *The Thing That Mattered Most: Scottish Poems for Children,* edited by Julie Johnstone (Edinburgh, UK: Black and White Publishing, 2006), p. 111.

Liz Lochhead (1947–). **IN THE MID-MIDWINTER.** In *Fugitive Colours* (Edinburgh, UK: Polygon, 2016), p. 127.

Charles Mackay (1814–1889): **THE WILL O' THE WISP,** p. 103.

Roger McGough (1937–). **TOMORROW HAS YOUR NAME ON IT.** In *Poetry Pie* (London, UK: Puffin Poetry, 2015), p. 150.

Walter de la Mare (1873–1956). **TIRED TIM,** 1912. In *Peacock Pie.* (London, UK: Constable & Co., Ltd), p. 20.

Edith Nesbit (1858–1934). **SONG,** 1886, p. 20.

Randy Newman (1943–). **SIMON SMITH AND HIS AMAZING DANCING BEAR.** *Sail Away* (Reprise Records, 1971), p. 69.

Edgar Allan Poe (1809–1849). **ANNABEL LEE,** 1849, p. 46.

Ezra Pound (1885–1972). **IN THE OLD AGE OF THE SOUL,** 1909. In *Personae.* (London, UK: Elkin Mathews), p. 138.

Otfried Preussler (1923–). **ALL SILVER.** In *The Little Water Spite,* 1956, p. 142.

Alison Prince (1931–2019). **RATS.** In *Flying Cat* (Arran, UK: Voice for Arran, 2013), p. 66.

Margery Rehman (Unknown–2015). **CARNIVAL EVENING,** p.124.

Annette Roeder (1968–). **SCAREDY-CATS.** © Annette Roeder, p. 96.

Karl Rühmann (1959–). **CARLITO CANNOT SLEEP,** p. 73; **SECRET OF THE STARS,** p. 146. © Karl Rühmann.

Sappho (625–576 BC). **FRAGMENT VI.** Translation by A. S. Kline, 2005, p. 74.

William Shakespeare (1564–1616). *The Tempest* Act III sc. 2, p. 41.

Anne Sexton (1928–1974). **HER KIND.** In *To Bedlam and Part Way Back* (Boston, US: Houghton Mifflin, 1960), p. 84.

Robert Louis Stevenson (1850–1894). **THE MOON,** 1885, p. 63.

Lord Alfred Tennyson (1809–1892). **THE PRINCESS: SWEET AND LOW,** 1850, p. 95.

Edward Thomas (1878–1917). **THE OWL,** 1915, p. 64.

Paul Verlaine (1844–1896). **CUPID FALLEN.** In *Paul Verlaine: Selected Poems,* translated by C. F. MacIntyre (Los Angeles, US: University of California Press at Berkeley, 1961), p. 58.

E. B. White (1899–1985). **DOG AROUND THE BLOCK,** 1932, p. 70.

Walt Whitman (1819–1892). **O CAPTAIN! MY CAPTAIN!** 1865, p. 27.

Jennifer Wong (dates unknown). **REIMAGINED GARDEN: ON JOHN SARGENT'S 'CARNATION, LILY, LILY, ROSE.'** In *Tate Etc.* Issue 20, 2010, p. 12.

Dorothy Wordsworth (1771–1855). **THE COTTAGER TO HER INFANT,** 1815, p. 34.

William Wordsworth (1770–1850). **A NIGHT IN JUNE,** 1802, p. 19.

Judith Wright (1915–2000). **RAINFOREST.** In *Collected Poems* (Australia: HarperCollins Publishers Australia, 1994), p. 41.

William Butler Yeats (1865–1939). **THE WILD SWANS AT COOLE,** 1917, p. 80.

Benjamin Zephaniah (1958–). **NATURE TRAIL.** In *Nature Trail* (London, UK: Orchard Books, 2020). Reproduced by permission of Orchard Books, an imprint of Hachette Children's Group, Carmelite House, 50 Victoria Embankment, London, EC4Y 0DZ, p. 87.

Notes from the English editors

This book offers you an irresistible combination—beautiful pictures and thoughtful words. It is based on a book that was very successful in Germany, so much so that the publishers wanted to offer a similar volume to English-speaking readers. What you are holding is the result—and ours was the happy job of choosing what should be included.

How to go about such a responsible role? We thought carefully about the images already in place—and with what kind of poems and short stories they might best be matched. Sometimes we took a picture literally (as in the poem on rats on pages 66–67). At other times we thought about what the image suggested and then racked our brains for what might best go with it (e.g. the dream picture on pages 108–9).

In the process, we found we remembered many more poems than we had imagined, sometimes from a very long time ago, and that trawling books and websites in search of writing to share was a real joy. We were determined to ensure a strong mixture—old and new, and from the full spectrum of society. We also wanted to mix them up, so you will find poets who wrote several centuries apart sitting next to each other.

How you read it is up to you. You might be drawn to particular images, to authors whose names you recognise—or perhaps to read all the short poems and extracts first. There is no "right" way to explore what is offered and we hope that all the writing, whether familiar or unfamiliar, will grow on you—in the same way that each time you return to a picture it can seem to have gained details you did not notice before.

Above all, everything in this book has been chosen with care. We really hope you will treasure the experience of sharing.

Alison and Matt

ACKNOWLEDGEMENTS

Alison would like to thank: two key English teachers who instilled a love of poetry—Mrs O'Neill from Ashlyns School and Miss Haddow from Berkhamsted School for Girls; Kelly Squires for her meticulous work on this book; Alasdair, Harriet, Jack, and Hamish for sharing their enjoyment of poetry, and particularly comic verse; Neil for his love of Gilbert and Sullivan and his ability to sing so many numbers from memory.

Matt would like to thank: Mum, for "The Little Dancers" and "The Owl" specifically, and more generally for the sense that all art, all literature is as much for me as anyone, a spirit that infuses this book and I hope all my work; Piers Pennington, for the loan of some writerly-eyes and for catching some real snafus (any uncaught ones are mine); and Saskia Nett for the on-the-spot translations—and the encouragement, on-tap. Danke!

© 2021 PRESTEL VERLAG, Munich · London · New York
A member of Penguin Random House Verlagsgruppe GmbH
Neumarkter Strasse 28 · 81673 Munich

Front cover: Henri Rousseau, *Carnival Evening*
Frontispiece: Maximilian Luce, *Camaret, Moonlight and Fishing Boats*
At the Height of the Moon originally is the title of a book by Eric Malpass.

Library of Congress Control Number: 2021937961
A CIP catalogue record for this book is available from the British Library.

Original concept and choice of artworks: Annette Roeder
Choice of poems in English: Alison Baverstock and Matt Cunningham
Additional research: Kelly Squires

Translations from the German (pages 23; 31–33; 73; 78; 88–90;
96–99; 104; 142–143; 146–149): Paul Kelly

EDITORIAL DIRECTION Doris Kutschbach
PROJECT MANAGEMENT Constanze Holler
PROOFREADING John Son
DESIGN AND LAYOUT Meike Sellier
PRODUCTION MANAGEMENT Susanne Hermann
SEPARATIONS Reproline Mediateam, Munich
PRINTING AND BINDING DZS Grafik, d.o.o., Ljubljana
PAPER Condat Périgord

Prestel Publishing compensates the CO_2 emissions produced from the making
of this book by supporting a reforestation project in Brazil. Find further
information on the project here: www.ClimatePartner.com/14044-1912-1001

Penguin Random House
Verlagsgruppe FSC® N001967
Printed in Slovenia

ISBN 978-3-7913-7480-2
WWW.PRESTEL.COM